THE
WISDOM
OF
LOVE
IN
BUSINESS

THE WISDOM OF LOVE IN BUSINESS

Transformational Tools to Achieve Entrepreneurial Success

KATHY GARDARIAN

with Tinker Lindsay

Published by Qualis International, Inc.

ISBN (paperback): 979-8-9899911-0-5
ISBN (ebook): 979-8-9899911-1-2

Book design and production by www.AuthorSuccess.com

Printed in the United States of America

To my beloved granddaughter Alyssa,
And to those who came before us,
who stand beside us,
And who will follow us.

CONTENTS

A Word About the Title

The ability to be flexible and open to change is key to any personal or professional success. Transformation sometimes means just that, literally changing the form of things. When I first published this book, six years ago, it was under the title *Feet to the Fire: Finding my Soul in Success*. While the details of my life's path as a female entrepreneur remain an important thread in this narrative, I have come to realize the message I most want to convey to those of you on your own entrepreneurial paths is both simpler, and more universal.

As Rumi puts it, "love is the bridge between you and everything." Love has proved to be my most powerful transformational tool, and love can be the lamp that lights the way to your own success.

And so I have changed the title, to better reflect my message. Farewell, with gratitude, *Feet to the Fire*. Welcome, *The Wisdom of Love in Business*.

May this book help you find success with your own transformational journey.

Kathy Gardarian

Someday, after mastering the winds, the waves,
the tides and gravity, we shall harness for
God the energies of love, and then, for a
second time in the history of the world,
man will have discovered fire.

—TEILHARD DE CHARDIN

**Life is made up
not of years, but of
moments.**

—ELI WEIZEL

FORWARD

For some women passion, commitment and determination are powerful tools for achieving personal and business success. For Kathy Gardarian, they describe a way of life.

Kathy walked into my life about twenty-eight years ago at the invitation of my partner, the world-renowned scholar and futurist Willis Harman. Willis believed Kathy's unique blend of personal ambition and spiritual awareness would mesh well with the basic tenets of the World Business Academy.

Kathy enrolled me in the story of her life's business challenge: to be a capable woman who could prove that her personal drive would create a highly successful company using openhearted love as her motivational tool, and defy the traditional male business influences who informed her she could not succeed without a man. They told her she would never make it. She knew they were wrong. Her life has been a concrete demonstration that a woman with evolved personal values can not only succeed, but do so beyond any normal expectation. More importantly, she lovingly went about her business in a unique way that honored her identification with "the feminine principle," and without recourse to traditional male stereotypes of how to achieve success in the marketplace.

Over the years I have sat with Kathy for hundreds of days, in an extraordinarily wide variety of circumstances, at meetings that have occurred on four separate continents. I have watched her and listened to her evoke the essence of the feminine as she addressed what otherwise would have been a "normal" business question. In fact, I personally recommended her to the chairman of the Vans Board of Directors for service in that company (she served ten years on that board) *specifically because* she could be counted upon to always bring the transcendent and the feminine into all her board deliberations.

Kathy has been a role model for business people of both genders, but particularly for young women who otherwise might falsely believe that the only path to success is to emulate the patriarchy, rather than to honor the feminine. Kathy gently yet firmly articulates her beliefs, and lives them fully in her life, both as a spiritual person and a successful professional. This book is a natural extension of her ongoing mission to invite and inspire others to do the same.

Rinaldo S. Brutoco
President, World Business Academy

An Invitation to my Readers

**Every moment I shape my destiny with a chisel.
I am the carpenter of my own soul.**

—JALALUDDIN RUMI

Friends have been urging me to write this book for years. "People need to hear your story, Kathy!" they'd tell me, whether at transformational business conferences, Sages and Scientists retreats, or tailgate parties at USC football games. But anyone who knows me well also knows that I can be stubborn, especially when I have some fear about something. I dig my heels in the sand. So it's no big surprise to them, or me, that this book has remained on the back burner until now.

What shifted? Mostly, the recognition that my beloved granddaughter, Alyssa, is not only growing up, she's growing up in a world that still for the most part operates as if stuck in an old paradigm. We can't keep doing this, pushing forward through life as if everything is fine. Leading with our egos, instead of our truest selves. Ignoring feminine principles while clinging to traditional models of success. There is a more evolved way to function, one that is not only kinder, but also more effective. I know, because I've experienced this to be true in my own business. I also know that Alyssa, and anyone else who feels a longing for a more conscious way to live and thrive, will be the change agents for this new way of being, and of doing. I want to reassure her, and you, dear reader, that it is not only possible, but practical, to lead with love instead of fear.

I invite you to join me as (once again!) I take a deep breath, set aside my resistance, and offer this tale in service to a new paradigm. Each of us has to find our own way, but that doesn't mean maps aren't helpful!

The truth is, I am blessed beyond measure. Every morning I carry a mug of coffee (organic Nicaraguan dark roast, with a squirt of whipped cream and a sprinkling of cinnamon) to the outside patio. There, I greet the two stately palms standing side by side: Isis and Osiris, my feminine and masculine reminders of the power of integrated energies. The three of us face the distant ocean, and I am filled with gratitude. And every night, I murmur thanks to the soft night air, and fall asleep humbled by the inner and outer riches that mark my day, and my world.

I did not start out this way. This is not a story about sainthood. As I often remind my son, it will never be said about me that I never complained. It's about making mistakes, learning, and growing. I had to learn how to be brave; how to hold my feet to the fire; how to invite deep change while tolerating acute discomfort. I had to keep my dreams and my ambition alive, in a world where strong women were often viewed with suspicion. I had to practice patience—not my strongest suit. Most of all, I had to maintain faith, and trust in the process, until I could finally reach a place not only of professional success, but of spiritual abundance.

How I found my way here is the subject of the book you hold in your hands.

I've always aimed high, and I understand all too well that ambition is a tricky business, especially for anyone as drawn to spirituality as they are to the marketplace. Navigating that confusing maze has been a lifelong challenge. I'd love to report that incorporating spirituality into my workplace was an easy process for me, and that giant neon signs pointed me toward my soul's destiny at every crossroads. I'd love to say that I never felt trapped, or divided, or confused. But I have felt all these things, more times than I can count. And the truth is, more often than not Spirit showed up in my life disguised as a problem.

Like that time I had to replace the sprayer on my garden hose. I wasn't looking for an answered prayer. I was looking for a new nozzle. My plants needed watering, and unless I did something about the busted sprayer, they'd wilt. I was less than thrilled about a trip to the hardware store, as it's never been my idea of fun. (Give me a shoe store any day of the week!) I don't especially like tools, nor do I enjoy using them, and a big part of me on that hot summer afternoon wanted to dig in my heels and wait for rain.

Reluctant or not, off I went to a building supplies store that had recently opened nearby, a little known retailer called The Home Depot that sold home and garden products. I was resigned to taking the next right action. I held my feet to the fire, so that my garden could grow.

The year was 1983, and that fateful trip to the hardware store changed the course of my life, not to mention the shape of my soul. Because of a faulty nozzle, a woman who barely owned a hammer became CEO of a wildly successful, worldwide distribution-and-supply company, whose main client, The Home Depot, became a wildly successful, worldwide mecca of the tool-belt crowd.

And people think the universe doesn't have a sense of humor!

Looking back, I can see how all the twists and turns of my lifelong quest for spiritual and material wholeness are contained in that long-ago trip to Home Depot. How often I've dug in my heels when it was time to do something new, outwardly hoping I'd find an easier way, inwardly knowing I wouldn't. How I've always, if reluctantly, realized that real change was up to me. My heart has had to learn to take action even as my head tells me to resist. My story is personal, as I trace the moments from past to present, connect the dots from then to now.

Business has always been my path, the furnace that forged me. But spiritual transformation is my passion, and my chosen vocation. Over time, I have come to understand that the two can go hand in hand: No. Not just *can*, but *should*.

I offer my story to those of you struggling for that same balance as you straddle two beams, one called Success, the other Spirit. Like you, I feared that ambition and soul were incompatible, and never the twain should meet. I tried to lead two separate lives for years, and often felt caught in the middle, frozen with fear, as a result. But fear is a curious word. It can stand for Forget Everything And Run, or Face Everything And Rise.

I grew up in a time when ambition was not considered a desirable feminine trait. Learning to succeed in the business world as a woman had, and still has, its specific challenges, to be sure. But this book is not just for women. It's for anyone who thirsts for a world in which Isis and Osiris—the masculine and the feminine—can both stand tall, side by side, hands clasped as they learn to navigate the boundless ocean of awareness and possibility.

Dear reader, if you long to cradle your success in a container of spirit, to bring feminine energy to the world of business, to shift your working paradigm from "dog-eat-dog" to "win-win," I know you. I know who you are, and how powerful you can be, because I stood where you stand. I stood there for a long time.

And then I took the first step.

Following in the Path of Love

I Too, have traveled upon the coldest of nights

and the hottest of days

just to catch a glimpse of your beauty and grace.

Roaming the earth

not knowing which direction to take or go

yet, I swear I have been upon this road

a thousand times or two before

and stumbled with exhaustion

that brought me to my knees.

But, nothing will keep me

from following in the path of Love... Nothing!

—GEORGI TUSCANI

1

SETTING THE STAGE

**The world is full of magic things,
patiently waiting for our senses to grow sharper.**

—WILLIAM BUTLER YEATS

I was born with one eye on the door, and the other peering inside for answers. Maybe I should blame the stars, or maybe it's simple math. According to numerologists, anyone born on the seventeenth contains a deep duality of purpose. On the one hand, we seek outer recognition, wealth and power. On the other, we quest for inner spiritual completion. If we are to find fulfillment, we must use whatever gifts we have to integrate these two worlds and bridge the gap between soul and success.

Sounds simple, right?

You know those anxiety dreams, where you're on stage and you realize you've not only forgotten all your lines, you're actually in the wrong play? That was my reality for the first eight years of my life. Somehow I'd been miscast in the role of a good little Italian-American girl, born in Buffalo, New York to a traditional, Catholic middle class family. I had an older brother who was seemingly perfect, a father who marched off to work every day in a suit and tie, and a stay-at-home mom who couldn't look at me without frowning. It was all a big mistake.

I would watch my father leave the house every morning, and wish I could follow him. What lay beyond the front door? Whatever it was, it had to be more exciting than staying at home! I would study my mother as she folded laundry or mopped the kitchen floor, her mouth a thin line of resentment, and wonder—is unhappiness really that necessary? She would catch me staring at her, and her frown would deepen. I knew without knowing that she not only felt miserable and trapped, but that somehow it was my fault. But how could that be? I just got here!

Only later would I learn that my mother had meticulously planned to escape her world, and marriage—toddler son in tow—when her careful plans were foiled at the last minute. Poised to head west and divorce my father, she discovered to her dismay that she was pregnant again. Pregnant, as it turned out, with me. A single mother trying to support one child in the late 1940's would be hard enough, but two? That would be madness. She shelved her dreams, and resigned herself to at least a few more years of cooking, cleaning, and ironing out the wrinkles of a life she was desperate to leave.

I guess you could say my own deep longing for a different, more authentic existence was baked into me while still in the womb.

Welcome or not, I arrived on January 17th, 1945. Capricorns are serious people, and I was no exception. I quickly sensed that my standing in our household was tenuous at best. My survival was at stake, and clearly no one was going to take care of this problem but me. So I set out to be flawless, right from the get-go, more perfect than my perfect big brother. The best little girl in Buffalo.

Buffalo was the coldest place in the world back then, in more ways than one. I think I wore thick woolen tights under my skirts nine months out of the year. Bundled up against hostile weather both inside the home and out, I functioned in over-drive long before I knew what that term even meant. Perfectionism was my model and my goal, and I was a fierce and serious little girl. But no matter how hard I tried, I was labeled the "difficult" child, while my brother Nick was "easy." I knew this to be false, even as a toddler, but it was also my reality, and therefore true.

Day after day I buckled up my sturdy Buster Browns—also known as my goody-two-shoes—and trotted after my mother. I tried with all my might to be helpful and therefore lovable. What else could I do?

If you are noticing the absence of my father in all this, that's because he was—mostly absent, I mean. When he wasn't working, he was fishing. Every weekend he would fill the kitchen sink with wall-eyed fish carcasses for my mother to gut and scale, her eyes averted. In those Post-war days, there was a scramble to re-clarify roles, and put Rosie the Riveter back into an apron where she belonged. Work was the husband's exclusive territory, home and family was the wife's, and the wall between the two was close to impenetrable. I kept my yearning to enter my father's world to myself.

While I might not have liked my mother's obvious resistance to me, I can certainly understand why she had it. I mean, look at our rough beginning together. But as I see it now, the deeper problem wasn't that she couldn't be there for me, but that she couldn't own her truth—admit *to herself* that every time she looked at me, instead of really seeing me, she saw her own shattered dreams of freedom. (She still can't admit this. The difference now is, I don't expect or need her to.)

Decades later, when I gave birth to my first and only child, my son Leo, I had a much greater appreciation for that mother-son bond. The connection was immediate, and more powerful than any other I had ever known. Giving birth to a new soul redefined everything for me. Of course I like to believe if I'd had a second child—a daughter, say—I would have loved her just as much, but I do understand my mother's almost primal connection to her firstborn.

I can also appreciate how much my mother struggled during those early years in Buffalo. She was in a marriage she didn't want, a life she didn't enjoy, and she had one too many children weighing her down. I get it, and I get her. But that doesn't mean I wasn't affected. These early influences shape us, for good and for ill. To this day, I have to watch my tendencies toward perfectionism and distrust. I've come to understand that in many ways my mother's frustrations with her own choices not only fueled my ambition, but created unnecessary resentment, especially as I grew more and more successful.

**Common sense is nothing more than a deposit of
prejudices laid down in the mind before
you reach eighteen.**

—Albert Einstein

Dear reader, I say all this not to complain, but to humbly offer this advice, based on my own experience—*Know your early drivers.*

For me, the deep need to be perfect, and therefore lovable, too often drove my future life choices—whether in love, or in business. I feared that life was essentially unfair, and that I would never be able to right that imbalance. Until I learned to identify and heal these hurts, I looked outside myself to repair them.

But success is an inside job.

How about you? When you think back to your earliest memories, what do you feel? Were any negative messages carved deep in your still-developing soul? What I know is this—We won't heal or evolve unless and until we are willing to shine a light on these hidden motivators, to really examine them.

I have a mantra that I rely on a lot: *You can't give what you don't have.* I've come to understand that many of us are often frustrated and depleted by our early choices and early drivers. When both our hands are in fists, how can we offer anything to ourselves, our family, or our world?

2

NIGHT AND DAY

We are asleep. But we wake up sometimes, just enough to know that we are dreaming.

—LUDWIG WITTGENSTEIN

My early years, while challenging, were also predictable, not to mention normal for the time. Mom stayed at home. Dad went to work. Family supper brought us all together briefly every evening. My mother was, at best, a disinterested cook. Our plates contained all the food groups, but everything came from cans and was leached of actual flavor. She dutifully included a single slice of white, spongy Wonder Bread, each piece placed on its own personal bread plate.

I would excuse myself to go to the bathroom, wadded bread tucked under my shirt. I had discovered a wooden door above the bathtub that opened into a wall space for easy access to the plumbing. I jammed the bread between the pipes, and flushed the toilet to complete the ruse. It was years before my mother discovered this secret cache of Wonder Bread, moldy evidence of my early rejection of blandness. And so my days marched along like worker ants, obedient, boring, one just like the other.

It was nighttime when the magic happened.

I'm not sure exactly when it started—my ritual communication with the unknown—but I know I was very young. After I fell asleep, I would wind up having conversations with lots of people. Not ghosts, exactly, but not completely real either, these entities occupied an in-between world. They would fill my bedroom, young, old, male, female, and we would talk about all manner of wondrous things. They were my dream companions. One in particular, a man named Abe, was a favorite, because he was so wise and kind. He was there all the time. We would discuss everything under the sun, or should I say, moon. Some years later, I would see his picture in a history book and realize he was not only famous, but he had a last name as well—Lincoln.

One day I asked my mother if I could leave the light on at night. I alluded to my nocturnal talks, although not by name.

"When I go to sleep at night, so many people come to visit me. I'd like it better if I could see the door."

My mother assumed I was having nightmares—Abraham Lincoln and friends fronting as Boogie Men—and she agreed to keep the light on. But the next morning, after my father passed my bedroom and noticed the still-burning bulb, he put his foot down.

"Waste of electricity," he announced.

His gruff pronouncement triggered a familiar iron set in my mother's jaw. After that, she made sure to get up early and switch off the light before he emerged from their bedroom. I was grateful, even if the act of rebellion was at least as much about her needs as mine.

These friendly, if restless, souls were my pals, and our nightly talks were comforting, especially when my parents' shouting matches rattled the rest of the house.

Young as I was, I knew without knowing that there existed another reality—one that didn't have to yell to be heard. There, living wasn't subject to rigid rules and didn't rely on suffering and strain to proceed. That state of being was full of ease, and joy, and more love than

I could ever imagine.

Even as a little girl, I was somehow able to distinguish between this deep connection to spirit, and our family's religion. The Catholic Church in the late nineteen-forties was very strong and very strict. My mother had her own problematic relationship with the church—as a little girl she was placed in a Catholic orphanage for a year, along with her four siblings. It was 1929, and her parents could not afford to keep them at home. Her time at the orphanage was harsh and lonely. The nuns were punitive—quick to use the ruler to keep everyone in line.

But Catholicism was also a fundamental support in her life, and the only spiritual home that she and my father knew. Both my brother and I were baptized as infants. We ate fish on Fridays, memorized the Lord's Prayer, and attended mass every Sunday.

Me being me, I naturally worked extra hard at being pious and blameless. But at church, as at home, I kept running up against things that made no sense. Whatever the priests said, it was as if I simultaneously heard a different voice in my heart, telling me what was and wasn't right or true. I memorized parts of the Catechism almost as soon as I learned to read, but notions like "sin" and "hell" simply didn't resonate.

I asked a lot of questions, questions about good and bad, life and death, right and wrong. What was grace? Why did some people get to have it, and others, not? Wasn't every person a child of God, no matter where he or she lived or what he or she looked like?

Naturally, this attitude didn't sit well with my Sunday school teachers.

"You can't ask questions like that," they would say, as if I might infect the other children with my impertinence. And so I saved them for my dream-world friends.

I raced through Catechism classes, made a First Confession, and took communion, all before my fifth birthday. When I look at the photograph of my First Communion Ceremony, I have to smile. I can see the suspicion in my eyes, and a stiff rebellion in my sturdy body that the dainty white ruffled dress can't disguise. Some part of me was already pretty sure this was not going to be my spiritual path!

Being a good little Catholic girl meant going to confession every Saturday morning, as well as showing up at church for Mass on Sunday. These rules were set in stone—like the Ten Commandments—and my breaking one of them very early on led to a soul-changing event.

As luck would have it, the year that I made my First Communion, both Christmas Day and New Year's Day landed on a Sunday. My brother, mother and I obediently attended Saturday morning confession December 24th, and Mass on Christmas Day. The following week, we again made it to confession New Year's Eve morning, but on New Year's Day, we stayed home. I can't remember why, only that it happened, and I felt a little guilty about it.

Five-year-olds as a rule don't have a lot to confess. ("I argued with my big brother." "I forgot to brush my teeth.") But that didn't mean the actual weekly event of Confession wasn't powerful, not to mention intimidating. I'd step inside a dark looming booth and close the door carefully behind me. Miles above was a little wooden grille, behind which loomed a hidden but scary Presence with a capital P. The Priest. The voice of God.

This particular morning was the Saturday after New Year's, and finally I had something significant to admit.

"Bless me Father, for I have sinned," I said. "I didn't go to church last Sunday."

The priest cleared his throat. I awaited my penance, so I could feel clean and perfect again.

"Young lady," I heard, "I want you to know that you have committed a mortal sin."

I knew this was a misstep, but a mortal sin? My eyes filled with contrite tears. But there was more, and worse, to come.

"When you are born, your heart is as white as snow," he said, his voice stern. "Every time you commit a mortal sin, God puts a black mark on your heart. When you die, if your heart has a lot of black marks, you will go straight to hell."

Whatever else he may have said to me, or instructed me to do, was lost in a swirl of panic. As soon as I could, I escaped from the confessional. I raced home to my mother. I was sobbing so hard I could barely form the words to recount what had happened. As I wailed into her lap, she silently, stiffly patted my back. I could tell she didn't think this was right, but she wasn't ready to leave the church of her own childhood—that was still a bridge too far. So she said nothing.

But even as my sobs became quiet sniffles, deep inside me a skeptical voice asked, "What kind of a religion *is* this?"

I decided two things then and there. First, if I ever had children, they would not be raised as Catholics. Second, I would put my children first. I would acknowledge them. Give them confidence and strength. Listen to their pain. Love them no matter what "mortal sins" the Church might decide they had committed.

Of course unconditional love requires more than simply vowing to be a better, more loving mother than my own was, but for then, it was enough. I stored those decisions away, and they gave me secret consolation.

I told no one about these "vows," just as I never mentioned the specifics of my vibrant dream world to my Sunday school teachers. I somehow knew they wouldn't approve of a little girl who disavowed the Church, not to mention held long conversations about spiritual matters with Abraham Lincoln and who knows who else? I didn't know the actual word for heresy, but I understood the concept.

These special visitors continued to people my dreams until one fateful night, the night everything changed and they evaporated like mist. I would not recall them until many years later.

I was sound asleep. Suddenly someone was shaking my arm.

"Mmph?"

"Get up. We're going to your grandmother's," my mother whispered.

Nick and I stumbled behind her and climbed into the back seat of the old family car, a bulbous Plymouth with musty upholstered seats. Soon we were speeding through the dark, my mother's hands gripping the wheel, my brother and me silent and baffled in the back seat. It was a quick drive to my grandparents' house. We pulled up in the dead of night, and my mother marched us inside, past our grim-faced grandparents.

Was this to be our home now? Nick and I exchanged confused looks as we trooped inside. No explanation given—and we didn't dare ask.

Within a few months my mother had found a job in the city of Rochester, sixty miles away. Once again we piled into the Plymouth, my mother at the wheel. This time she moved us into our own place, part of a new subdivision—a boxy unfurnished house set at the edge of a large patch of woods. We knew no one in Rochester, and so had nowhere to go. I would invade my mothers closet and slip into a pair of her high heels. Ducking out the back door, I'd traipse though the mossy trees, pretending to be a grown-up person. Someone in charge. Someone whose life wasn't uprooted over and over again without warning.

After that, every other weekend my mother would deposit my brother and me onto a big blue Rochester transit bus. The driver soon knew to thumb me to the far back, where I was certain to throw up at least once. We would spend an awkward, mostly silent day with my father—who no doubt wished he were fishing—then take the long nauseous ride back to our strange new home.

Moving to Rochester was Phase One of my mother's master plan of escape. In those days, a period of physical separation—non-cohabitation was the legal term—was a necessary first step to leaving New York, not to mention her marriage.

Two years later, when I was eight, my mother packed up the Plymouth one final time with Nick, me, and all our earthly possessions. This time we headed west. She was chasing down what came to be known as a "migratory divorce." New York in the early 1950's had some of the strictest divorce laws in the country, especially for women. There was no such thing as no-fault, and basically, the only acceptable ground for divorce was adultery, a non-starter for my mother. Add to that the fact that the strict New York Catholic Diocese did not recognize divorce for any reason whatsoever, and you had a recipe for lifelong marital misery unless you somehow managed to get out of Dodge.

In California, "cruelty" was a second, acceptable ground for divorce, and the definition for cruelty could be stretched—and often was—to include simple incompatibility. This was especially true when husband and wife had lived in two separate locations for a significant length of time. So while the actual infliction of pain might be absent, claiming "cruelty" was not only cheaper, but also far less mortifying than staging a fake adulterous encounter.

I didn't understand any of this at the time. All I knew was divorce would mean a black mark on my poor mother's heart the width of the Grand Canyon.

She must really need to do it.

We drove cross-country all day, and spent our nights in cheap motel rooms with scratchy sheets and stained walls that reeked of bleach and cigarette smoke. We ate in greasy diners and the occasional Howard Johnson's for a special treat. I watched my mother counting out coins, her forehead furrowed as she pored over the checks.

Where are you taking us? Will I like it? Will you finally be happy?

One warm summer evening we pulled in front of an apartment complex, a pastel box of stacked windows, each with its own tiny balcony.

"Here we are," my mother said. "Manhattan Beach."

I climbed out of the back seat, my legs stiff from hours of sitting. My nose wrinkled at the unfamiliar tangy air, salted with the sea. I inhaled the scent of perfumed trees, fragrant and heady.

It smelled like freedom.

My brother and I ran the two blocks to a wide stretch of beach. I skidded to a stop. The white sand unrolled for miles in both directions. Before me danced the turquoise and green wavelets of the Pacific Ocean. Beyond, a smoky blue horizon reached to forever. Cold, grey, suffocating Buffalo lay a lifetime behind me. Something loosened in my chest, as I tasted a new kind of hope.

Heaven was real. I was home.

**A self is made, not given.
It is an active and creative process of attending a life
that must be heard, shaped, seen, said aloud into the
world, finally enacted and woven into the lives of others.**

—Barbara Myerhoff

Dear reader, it's hard but so important to *question inherited beliefs,* to allow our own intuition to lead the way. We are handed down so many undisputed principles when we are young. We take them to be true, to be reality, when in fact they themselves have probably been acquired without question, and unconsciously.

I inherited notions of guilt and sin, not to mention what was and wasn't okay for women to feel and want. How about you? What beliefs were handed down to you? Which ones felt right and true? Which did you have to let go?

Eventually we have to open our eyes and ears, make up our own minds. Otherwise we are simply sleepwalking our way through life, bolstered by borrowed notions. This is true both personally and professionally!

Believe me, I know how scary challenging old ideas can be, but we must dare to question these inherited systems. We all have them! Look for where they resonate, using intuition like a divining rod. Once we learn to listen to and trust our inner voice, we can keep whatever works for us, and let go of the rest, with gratitude and a gentle farewell bow.

3

GETTING WARMER

Truth cannot be taught, but it is quickly recognized by the person ready to discover it.

—BARRY LONG

Our little family of three landed in Manhattan Beach on the crest of a new wave of growth and optimism. The population in these Southern California ocean side communities more than doubled between 1950 and 1960 as families like mine migrated west in search of more and better opportunities.

In 1952, the year before we pulled up in front of the Manhattan Beach apartment building, city planners planted an exciting new signpost on the edge of what had been a small municipal airfield. "L. A. International Airport," it proclaimed, a painted arrow pointing toward the endless opportunities that lay ahead in the form of hundreds of flights and multiple runways and terminals.

Like me, this part of the world was ripe and ready to blossom.

While still in Rochester, my mother had somehow managed to secure a position at Douglas Aircraft Company in Long Beach, one of the numerous aerospace manufacturers that dotted the southern pacific coast. It was brave of her, to leave what was safe and familiar, two young children in tow. Whenever I want to judge her harshly, I remember the courage it took to make this westward trek.

She would rise early every morning and leave for work, exhausted but with a spring in her step. She urged the old Plymouth to Long Beach, thankfully a short commute. As a single mother, she still struggled to come out even at the end of every month, and we knew not to bother her on bill night. Dinner was more often than not *Pasta e Fagioli*—the frugal but hearty meal of our Italian peasant ancestors. My mother's version meant overcooked elbow macaroni mixed with a can of white beans, a slice of white bread on the side, and nowhere in our apartment for me to hide it.

My stomach experienced first hand what struggling financially as a single mother meant, prompting another vow. I would have a stable, lucrative career one day. More early drivers kicked in—Success was up to me, no matter what. Marriage was not a trustworthy institution. Only a fool would put their wellbeing into another person's hands.

One day, I'll make my own money, I thought, although that was as far as it got. The fact is, girls like me were supposed to want husbands, not careers.

Up until now, I had followed every rule, and walked a narrow line. Something about this new mix of California sunshine and a fresh start activated an unfamiliar sensation in me, part fear, part anticipation. In a land of endless horizons, maybe anything was possible, even for a girl.

I can't say I loved my new elementary school. Everyone there was like family to each other. As an incoming third-grader, I was automatically labeled an interloper. I had thick, mahogany brown hair, hazel eyes, and my voice, even back then, was deep and Lana Turner low. I was a misfit, nothing like a typical sun-bleached surfer gal, though I took to Southern California like one.

Nick hated his new school as well. We hatched a plan for playing hooky, an occasional reprieve when we needed a break. On those days, after our mother left for work, we would pull the shades in our apartment and hunker down. We'd grab cans of soda from the ice box and pull out the board games. It was a delightful escape, if short-lived.

One day, truant officers were dispatched to our apartment. They pounded on the door, trying to peer inside. We scrambled to the back bedroom and climbed to the top section of the closet. Holding our breaths, we pressed deep behind the hanging dresses and coats. We thought we were so smart!

Unfortunately, the super had a key and let the truant officers inside. More unfortunately, that day we were out of soda, and Nick had the wise idea to open two cans of beer instead.

We stayed absolutely still in our bedroom hideaway but the beer and half-played Monopoly game gave us away. The officers soon discovered our hidey-hole, and my mother got the call, the "Your children have been ditching classes and drinking" type of call. I've never seen her so angry—with Nick, as well as me. For once, he and I were on the same side, partners in crime. She straightened us out, our days of playing hooky came to a screeching halt, and the moment of camaraderie passed.

On weekends, and after school, I couldn't get enough of the ocean, the rolling dunes and sparkling wavelets. I'd gaze at the occasional airplane overhead, wings glinting as it skimmed the rim of blue. The spark of joyful adventure was ignited, a spark that would later fuel trips around the globe.

One day, I promised myself, one day I will be on one of those airplanes.

My inner life was shifting as well, and when I was twelve, I took my first spiritual stand. I had renewed Catechism classes at our new church, and soon it was time for me to be confirmed. Confirmation, my teacher informed me, was the completion of the Catholic sacraments of baptism, penance, and communion. A time when the faithful were sealed with the gift of the Holy Spirit.

It sounded pretty final to me.

That Sunday I walked into my mother's bedroom, took a deep breath, and told her, No. No more catechism class. No more confession. No more Holy Communion. I admitted that I had never lost my early distaste for the rigid judgment of the Catholic Church. Nothing about it felt life affirming to me. If God is love, I asked her, where is that love? I'm sorry, I concluded, but I no longer choose to participate.

To my mother's eternal credit, she didn't object. Maybe the endless summers had started to thaw her out as well. More likely, it was the fact that along with her divorce came instant excommunication from the Catholic Church. The decision was out of her hands. She, too, could finally say good riddance.

That didn't mean I stopped searching for a spiritual home. If anything, my hunger for soulful community had only grown stronger with time. I became a serial church-hopper—the fact is, if you were a seeker of higher truths in the late fifties and early sixties there wasn't anywhere else to go! I tagged along with various friends, taste-testing their different religious communities to see if my soul fit in. I tried on everything. Lutherans, Episcopalians, Baptists, Holy Rollers. I became enamored with the Mormon Church—well, sort of. I stayed on at their place of worship for months past its sell-by date because I had a huge crush on the Bishop's son. The Church of Latter-Day Saints might not have been the right inner match, but the Bishop's son suited my outer needs just fine.

By this time I had transitioned to Airport Junior High, and as if inspired by the name, I took off. Everyone wanted to be my friend. I truly became "a part of" instead of "apart from." I entered Westchester High School in Marina del Rey on top of the world. I was popular. I was smart. I had friends galore. I flirted with boys named Howie and Bink, and oh, that Rudy Lisardi, with his slicked-back hair and smoky eyes. Rudy was a gymnast, with great legs and a killer smile. *Kathy Lisardi*—that had a nice ring to it.

To an outside observer, my life was a joyous merry-go-round of fun and success. But as anyone riding a merry-go-round will tell you, it's impossible to experience stillness unless and until the carousel stops spinning.

Home life, too, had improved. When I turned fifteen, my mother met a wonderful man at work, Clayton. Soon they were "an item," and before long they were married. Clayton was six years younger than my mother, and therefore much groovier in my eyes. An engineer, he was by nature both curious and patient. He would sit with me for hours helping decipher algebraic equations and clarify principles of physics and chemistry. His presence almost made us seem like a normal family.

Soon after Clayton and my mother married, the four of us returned to New York to visit my grandparents. One afternoon my mother dropped off my brother and me at our old house, where my father still lived. We visited with his side of the family—relatives I hadn't seen in close to a decade. As the day grew late, I moved outside to sit on the front stoop, a little overwhelmed by it all. My father joined me. He was still as handsome and dapper as in my memories—dark suit, white shirt, knotted tie and polished shoes, fedora perched on his head. He questioned me about school, about friends, about the ocean. We talked about a lot of things, everything except my new stepfather. It was the last time I would see my dad— he died nine short years later.

Clayton grew up on a farm in Nebraska, impossibly exotic to this city girl. He decided to introduce us to all the National Parks, and took the family on a series of camping "vacations"—an experience I loved in theory, if not in practice. Those trips would prove to be the one and only time I slept outdoors in a tent. (Give me clean sheets and room service any time!) I had moved on from toys to boys, and was much more interested in dancing the mashed potato than roasting a marshmallow.

More than anything else, Clayton made my mother happy. I took note, and felt thankful, for I still seemed to mostly bring her unease, much as I tried to please.

Overdrive takes its own toll, and no matter how hard I smiled as I trotted from class to class and crush to crush, my eyes told a different story. I was elected first runner up for Winter Wonderland Queen, and my yearbook photograph presents an interesting portrait of me at that time. The narrow spaghetti straps of my white gown show off a youthful pair of shoulders, and my dark, chin-length pageboy frames the unblemished complexion of a pretty seventeen-year-old. But my eyes! They stare directly into the camera—ancient, fierce and determined. They are the eyes of a girl with the weight of the world on her shoulders, burdened beyond her years.

Lighten up, I want to tell her. It's not so bad!

Senior year, along with early morning choir practice, and representing the Girl's League, and church-hopping, and making honor role, and obsessing over Rudy Lisardi, and getting my driver's license, and, and, and, I ran for President of the Arondas. The Arondas was a subgroup of my high school's girls-only G.A.L.S. Club (Gabrinians, Arondas, Lydians and Shereens). We all attended weekly meetings, an identical herd of teeny-boppers with bobbed hair, matching red sleeveless v-necked sweaters—embroidered insignia front and left—prim Peter Pan collared blouses and knee-length pleated skirts.

The evening of the Club elections, my friend Julie arrived at the door so she and I could drive to the event together. My mother popped outside to say hello. The night was chilly, and I shivered in my carefully selected matching peach-colored skirt and cardigan. I ran back inside to grab a jacket. When I returned, my mother do-si-do'd around me without a word and disappeared in the house.

A curious look crossed Julie's face.

"What?" I asked.

"Nothing," she said, hooking elbows with me. "Hurry. We don't want to be late."

"And the new president is…"

They announced my name.

I walked past applauding friends to accept the president's gavel, my brain dazed. *I don't believe it. I won. I won.* I floated home and danced upstairs, gavel in hand.

"Mom?"

She was in the bedroom, transferring a stack of folded laundry into a dresser drawer.

"Guess what?" I said to her bent back. "I won! I'm the new president of the Arondas!"

She swiveled to face me. "I know," she said, her face unreadable. "Julie told me before you left." She returned to her work.

But I was in High School now, and I had learned a few things about taking care of myself. I did what I've been doing a version of ever since. I ran to my next-door neighbors to tell them the news.

"Isn't that wonderful, Kathy!" the mom of the house said, as her daughter beamed beside her. "Congratulations. We're so proud of you."

It was almost enough, and so much better than nothing.

The truth is, whether as Winter Wonderland princess or GALS Club President, I was frantically looking for that external thing to fix me, that person or place or prize or praise that would prove once and for all that I mattered. Some part of me kept crying out, Look, everyone! I'm getting straight A's! I have friends! I'm in the A Cappella Choir! Don't look there, look over here! I can do this! I can fix this!

My soul starved for something, but I didn't yet know what. Surely success would bridge that gap.

Blessed is the influence of one true, loving, human soul on another.

—George Eliot

Dear reader, you are so precious. *Go where the love is.* Seek out and embrace encouragement and support where you can, especially when you are still trying to find your own way. No one can tell us who we are meant to be, or where our purpose lies, but finding people who believe in us makes that journey seem possible. The road to wisdom is personal, but collective support can smooth the way. Anyone who has ever run a marathon will tell you—the crowds cheering from the sidelines make it possible to push through any walls.

Everyone deserves accolades and acceptance. We are all born in light, and worthy of love. Find other mothers, other mentors. I promise you they are out there, waiting to be found.

4

TAKING OFF

—STEVIE NICKS

By the time graduation rolled around, I was more than ready to move on—so that I could move out. I'd park by the fenced bean fields adjacent to the airport, gaze at the planes rising like wild geese and heading for parts unknown, and dream of one day becoming an airline stewardess. How else could an ambitious girl see the world?

My first paying job was less glamorous—I was a sacker at Fedco, a giant big-box store recently opened near our home. Within weeks, I was upgraded to checker. One morning, a fellow-checker pulled me aside, as if she had a state secret to share.

"New guy starting tomorrow," she confided. "His name is Leo. You're going to really like him."

I shrugged it off. Unless he was Rudy Lisardi's clone, I wasn't interested.

Sure enough, the next day found a new guy was working in front of me at the checkout stand. From the back, he looked tall and way too skinny.

Nope. Not my taste.

He turned to look at me and smiled.

Okay, handsome.

Then he winked.

And he has swagger.

For three months Leo pressed me to go out with him. I finally caved, even though I wasn't sure a Fedco sacker with an attitude was my ultimate destiny. Then I saw his car—a refurbished red Thunderbird, complete with a Corvette engine he'd installed himself.

Uh oh.

He drove me to dinner way too fast, and I liked that, too.

Once we kissed, I was toast.

Leo was utterly charming when he wasn't being totally annoying. He was devoted to me—he even joined me in my ongoing search for a church-home. We agreed together that the Presbyterian Church was banal enough to suit—they used the best of the bible but otherwise were remarkably edict-free.

I was attending UCLA, Leo, Pierce College. Our relationship was as sporadic as it was passionate. As much as Leo insisted he loved me and couldn't live without me, he wouldn't commit to anything more than a good time. When we were on, we were inseparable. When we were off, I would date other men with fabulous résumés—much more suitable and willing to pop the question—and wonder what Leo was doing.

I filled my UCLA schedule with classes in business and psychology. The former fed my early yearning for a career. The study of business gave me a glimpse into my absent father's intriguing world, the one that lay beyond the front door when I was little, and still seemed exotic and just out of reach now. The hole he left contained its own magnetic force, and I longed to tap into that power.

Psychology classes were the closest I could get to understanding how the mind worked, and where ones soul might fit in. This longing still sang to me like a Siren—Spirit wouldn't let me go.

No one else I knew was haunted by the need to connect the spiritual with the practical. And I still needed to identify some sort of long-term paying job.

One of my between-Leo beaus was an accounting major from USC. He lived on a designated floor for students enrolled in dentistry school. The boys were all acquiring DDS degrees, while the girls, per usual, were expected to set their sights slightly lower. Still, Dental Hygienists made a lot more per hour than checkers at Fedco. I'd never stopped looking for a career that would allow me financial freedom—maybe cleaning teeth was the answer. I set aside my innate squeamishness and signed up for a required pre-test to determine manual dexterity. The process involved a lump of soft wax, a variety of tiny sharp-edged tools, and scraping.

To say I failed the "gum gardener" test is a spectacular understatement. Clearly, I would ruin far more mouths than I would clean. Dental hygienist was no longer an option.

The USC boyfriend proved equally wrong for me, at least in my mind at the time. Looking back, he was not only lovely, but a great listener. He also owned a red Corvette, which he offered to me if I'd marry him! While we were together, as was my pattern, his interests became my interests, his friends my friends, his football team my football team. To this day, I am an avid Trojans fan because of this discerning man. No Bruins paraphernalia in my house! Finding a football team to love—including a coach, Pete Carroll, who still serves as an inspirational mentor—was his greatest gift to me.

I next turned to law as a possible profession, but their pre-test, too, revealed I had little aptitude for thinking like a lawyer. (To which I now say, thank goodness!)

Meanwhile, I continued to inhale my psychology classes. My affinity for it was telling. I've never lost the deep desire to heal internal wounds and foster growth, and have always tried to practice these principles, with or without the title of psychologist. I might be one today, had not marriage interrupted my studies.

My most serious suitor during that time—Ronald Skaggs—was the son of the founding partner of Safeway. Ronnie was older by several years, and wore his wealth like a loose garment. He was not only handsome, but my landlord—he actually owned the apartment building where my friends and I rented our student apartment. He was also more than ready to settle down.

One day he pulled out a soft cloth pouch and told me to open my hand. He poured a stream of loose, uncut diamonds into my palm and asked me to choose my favorite stone for the engagement ring.

I was shocked. I told him I needed more time.

He whisked me to a stunning, brand new house in the hills of Bel Air complete with pool, view, and a For Sale sign.

"Our future home," he said. "Just imagine how great it will be, Kathy. You can invite all your friends over, any time you want."

Yeah, I thought. But I probably can't invite Leo.

Again, I postponed my answer.

I'd obviously let slip my fondness for sports cars, because the next time Ronnie showed up, it was in a bright yellow Corvette, dealer plates still on. He handed me the key.

"Let's take it for a spin," he said.

This time, I didn't hesitate. I knew exactly where we should go.

Anyone who owned a cool car with loud pipes in the Del Rey area hung out at the Wich Stand on Slauson Avenue—it was the place to be when you wanted to show off your sheet metal. The Stand was hard to miss. A sharp spire jutted out of the canted roof like a rocket, and flat, satellite-shaped umbrellas dotted the small outdoor tables. The overall effect was tacky, trying really hard to be futuristic, but nobody cared. It was hot-rodder heaven. Even the Beach Boys, our local gods of song, immortalized the Wich Stand with its own sunny song. The Stand was a drive-in diner—drive-ins were popping up everywhere at the time—and the waitresses would pull aside each car in their short shorts and roller skates, trays balanced on one hand.

More than anything else, though, the Stand was a mecca for bad boys, and that included my favorite one.

Call it fate, or call it synchrony, but when I pulled up in the brand new Corvette, there was Leo in his red T-bird, parked in the next slot. Leo later told me that the sight of me in that bright yellow 'vette—Ronnie riding shotgun—got through to him as nothing else had.

"I knew I'd lose you if I didn't get off the fence," he admitted.

I shed Ronnie and his myriad gifts, and my college life, without a second thought. Leo was the one, the best one for me. I just loved him. And loving Leo meant wanting to be his wife.

We married in the Presbyterian Church in October of 1965, a few months before my twenty-first birthday. I took his last name. From now on, I would be Kathy Gardarian. Happily ever after couldn't come fast enough for me.

But like any perception based on illusion, this idealized story of ours couldn't last. When I found that I was pregnant, I clung to the hope that a baby would cement our connection, a connection that felt more fragile with every passing day. Instead, having a baby pulled the blinders from my eyes. It revealed the cracks in our fantasy, and unmasked a truer version of both of us. That truth was quite a shock.

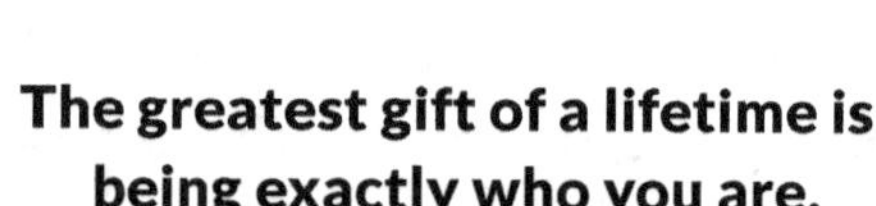

The greatest gift of a lifetime is being exactly who you are.
—Joseph Campbell

Dear reader, the Oracle at Delphi said it first and best. *Know Thyself.* Like all timeless truths, it has never lost the power to transform. Remember earlier when I suggested we can't give what we don't have? Let me now offer its kissing cousin—*You can't choose what you don't know.*

I met Leo when I was barely seventeen, and married him three and a half years later. I didn't know myself, I didn't know Leo, and I certainly didn't know life. My "picker" wasn't broken, it was nonexistent!

Leo and I shadow-danced an awkward waltz of pretending. Neither of us really saw the other—how could we, when we couldn't see ourselves?—and both of us clung to the belief that we were perfectly matched. For me, "loving" seemed always to morph into "deferring." I would lose myself in every relationship, setting aside my own wants and needs. Like others born into a sense of lack, it was a behavior I had to keep un-learning.

I had to look inside, to explore and accept my own deepest needs and beliefs in order to meet others on equal ground.

And you? In what ways have you had to expand your knowledge of yourself? How has that journey to greater self-awareness affected your world, and your work?

5

DARING TO DREAM

**Keep some room in your heart
for the unimaginable.**

—MARY OLIVER

They placed the warm tiny bundle into my arms. I looked down. A pair of eyes met mine, infant eyes, as wise and innocent as dawn. *You again…*

My heartbeat slowed to a stop. Who was this little soul? How had he come to be here, so perfect, so beautiful? Why did I feel as if we'd known each other forever? His fingers were delicate, each nail a translucent crescent. I touched his palm, and he curled his fist around my forefinger. His steady gaze was the embodiment of trust and acceptance. He was my son, and I was his mother.

Just like that, I grew up.

I felt it all, in that first moment with my baby boy, Leo. How I would never put another bite of food into my mouth without first making sure he was fed. How clothing him, protecting him, nurturing him and supporting him now came before everything else. The power of this maternal force acted like a clarifying agent, distilling my vague sense of unease into certainty. My newborn had needs. My job was to meet them.

The first year of marriage had been hard—like waking into a parallel world where everything seemed the same but nothing was quite right. Leo and I had moved into our own apartment in Huntington Beach. He was still in school, searching for a career that suited, and we struggled to pay the rent. Every once in a while, I would remember that Bel Air house and bright yellow Corvette, but Leo was the love of my life. We'd make it work. We had to.

For months, I'd tried my best to be a housewife, but once I'd organized the socks for the umpteenth time, I would find myself longing for something else, *anything* else to happen. In my young bride's mind, Leo and I were equal partners, and our life together would reflect that balanced equation. In reality, I was stronger than he was—more forceful, more driven, more organized. But nothing in my social upbringing or religious training had a place for that dynamic. No wonder I felt so confused.

My mother and Clayton were still happily married, and deeply in love. They wanted to share the experience of raising their own child, and adopted four-month-old Jeff when my Leo was only a month old himself. We raised our babies together, and to this day they are as close as any siblings. Clayton passed along his love of the outdoors to the two boys, and Leo and Jeff shared many joyful summers fishing and camping out under the stars.

Giving birth to my son had other, perhaps unintended, consequences. It not only galvanized me but also exacerbated Leo's and my differences. For me, motherhood was a call to arms. I set out once again to find a steady job, so I could provide for our son. I scoured the wanted pages, and saw an opening for a receptionist at, irony of ironies, a dental practice down the street.

I would work there for the next ten years.

I was still singularly ill suited for certain aspects of the job—collecting mouth guards from patients, for example. I'd never lost my squeamishness. But the business side of things? That was a different matter. I loved setting up patient systems, organizing schedules, streamlining the flow of appointments. Hand me a ledger to balance, and I was happy. I especially appreciated getting a steady paycheck, knowing that I was taking care of little Leo's needs. My husband grew more and more unclear about his place and purpose in life. Me? I was too busy to be confused. Every waking hour was spent either working, or caring for our son. I loved Leo fiercely, and would do anything for him. But like an old familiar refrain, a part of me started to wonder again—Is this it? Should my soul feel this dry, my heart this lonely? I felt stuck. Stuck in the wrong job. Stuck in the wrong marriage. Stuck in the wrong life.

I had become my mother.

Not only that, while I might have left the Catholic Church years earlier, the guilt those early priests instilled in me truly was the gift that kept on giving. The need to be a "good girl" was primal, the marrow in my bones. Divorce did not seem like an option.

Until one day it did.

After seven years of trying, I had finally had enough. I told Leo I was done—*we* were done.

"It's over. I'm sorry. I don't trust you," I said. I remember him looking at me in disbelief.

"But I love you. If I'd known I would lose you, I would have behaved differently," he said. As if his choices were somehow my responsibility.

My son was five years old—the same age I was when my mother made the identical choice. How hard we try to escape past patterns. How often we repeat them.

I filed for a divorce. The sky did not fall.

**And if you don't love me now,
you will never love me again.
I can still hear you saying you
would never break the chain.**

—Fleetwood Mac

Dear reader, only when we *recognize dysfunctional systems* can we make healthier choices. What a revelation this was to me—dysfunctional systems replicate dysfunctional systems!

I chose the exact partner to reenact my parent's past, no matter that Leo and I both seemed so different from them. Luckily, I also eventually accessed the same courage that my mother had to find in order to break that chain. But I might have saved myself years of struggle had I truly understood the dysfunctional systems in which I was raised. And not just personal—cultural, spiritual, and professional!

We have to first recognize dysfunction, whether personal, spiritual, or professional, before we can release it. Have you had this experience? Have you explored dysfunction with curiosity—gazed with unblinking eyes on the personal and cultural ideas that serve as your incubators? If we don't recognize these fault lines, we are bound to make the same painful choices. But happily, once we identify the flaws in our innate patterns of upbringing, we can let them go, and move into a new way of being, one in alignment with who we really are.

6

One Foot In, One Foot Out

**Fear is powerful, but your soul is unafraid.
Find your soul and it will dissolve your suffering.**

—DEEPAK CHOPRA

Sometimes I think fear should be my middle name. The moment our divorce was official, Leo began a fresh campaign—to persuade me to remarry him. And all my finger-shaking judgers—the ones behind the high grille in the dark confession booth of my mind—raised their voices to join his, stronger than ever.

Who are you to deprive your young son of his father?

Leo loves you, shouldn't that be enough?

And by the way, little missy, nice girls don't get divorced.

Leo came to me with a new proposal. "If you won't remarry me, how about we buy a bigger place together and live in it as a family? We still have the same last name. No one even needs to know we're divorced."

Divorce was still rare, if not frowned upon back then, and much as I wanted to be free of Catholic guilt, I hadn't yet erased the stain of it on my heart.

We bought a condominium in Lake Forest in Orange County, and true to his promise, Leo worked very hard at being the husband I had always wanted. A year passed. Two. I went to work at the same job, came home to the same house, slept under the same roof with the same man. Although our marriage might not be legally binding, the ties that bound us were just as tight.

But I would leave our bed at night and go into the living room to cry. I felt betrayed—but not by Leo anymore.

By me.

I loved him, but I wasn't in love with him. I couldn't re-find the trust. I didn't want to be his wife.

And every morning, I'd mask my sorrow with make-up and step back into my routine, as day, followed day, followed day.

Suddenly I was twenty-nine years old, and wedged in so tight I could no longer breathe. Leaving this man who loved me was still a terrifying prospect, and a part of me thought I might not survive. But I was already wasting away. Really, what did I have to lose?

I asked Leo to move out.

He paused by the front door, surrounded by boxes and bags—his portion of our life together. Night had fallen, and our son was already asleep.

"I have two things to say to you." Leo's voice was hard and certain. "One, you will never find anyone that will love you as I do. And two, you'll never make it financially without me."

He knew me so well. The arrows he let loose flew straight and true, piercing my two most vulnerable spots—my lovability, and my ability to support our son on my own.

I sat on the living-room sofa for hours, surrounded by deepening shadows. The house was silent, but not my mind.

What if he's right? WHAT IF HE'S RIGHT?

Fear took on a shape and settled on the couch to my left—a dark metallic presence, unbending, like a pillar of steel. I shifted away, but the pillar stuck close to my side.

Go away, I thought.

Sorry. Not gonna be that easy, Fear answered.

I stood up. I turned on the living-room lights. Time to be brave. Time to try a little more honesty and authenticity. Time to practice trust in my own God-given abilities. I walked into my bedroom, trailed by my new best friends, Fear and Guilt. It was going to be crowded in bed tonight. That was okay. I could handle it.

A few weeks later, I met a friend for lunch, someone who had known me for a long time. In the past, our meals had consisted of alternating tales of woe, interspersed with plaintive pleas for things to change.

This lunch was different. Not from my side—I was still wracked with guilt over kicking Leo out, and filled with fear about the future. But my friend radiated a new sense of purpose. He seemed to have an awful lot of clarity all of a sudden. He talked about taking responsibility for his actions—how the word itself meant an *ability to respond appropriately*. And it wasn't just talk—he'd made some actual moves, concrete changes with measurable results.

What was going on?

My friend laid it out. He'd attended a training course over a couple of weekends—an intense series of sessions developed by a man called Werner Erhard. I hadn't heard of EST, or this guy Erhard, but I was intrigued. Something about this process resonated.

A few nights later I found myself at an evening gathering, supposedly just an un-pressured introduction to Erhard's ideas. I sat at the back of a crowded hotel ballroom, arms crossed, as a couple of bright-eyed and fervent enthusiasts talked of experiencing life-changing personal shifts and massive transformations of consciousness. I knew a heavy-duty sales pitch when I heard one, and they were selling this training a little too hard. Thanks, I thought, but no thanks.

I would let my friend be the guinea pig.

Albert Einstein once wrote, "Setting the example is not the main means of influencing another, it is the *only* means." Six months later

I was thirty years old. It was not a happy birthday. I was still trapped inside the wrestling ring, pinned in place by the same pair of opponents, Guilt and Fear. Occasionally Blame showed up on the sidelines, just to jeer. Meanwhile, my friend had a new job, a new relationship, and a brand new lease on life.

I picked up the phone, my heart pounding.

"I think I might be ready to take that training," I said.

"Good," he said. "Time to get off the guilt fence."

I know there are those who found EST to be too cult-like and controlling. For me, entering their arena was like moving from an arid desert into a lush and fragrant garden. I couldn't get enough of this new way of perceiving things, a path that embraced both intuition and accountability. These people didn't see spiritual growth and personal success as opposing forces, but as natural allies.

For the first time, I was exposed to Eastern philosophies—Hinduism, Zen Buddhism, notions of higher states of consciousness and multiple lifetimes and masculine and feminine energies. The memory of my nighttime friends returned, and I no longer felt crazy for communing with Abraham Lincoln as a little girl, or naïve for believing that God-consciousness didn't have to be exclusive and judgmental.

Best of all, I was given tools to forgive myself and forgive Leo, so I could finally step into my own shoes and move on.

He and I had made a beautiful son. What a fine thing we did together!

EST gave me permission to trust myself. To recognize that from the moment I could form thoughts, a still small voice had chimed in when things felt off-kilter or out of whack. This was the intuitive voice that whispered as the priest berated me, "What kind of religion *is* this?" This inner presence challenged the truth behind my mother's seeming rejection of me. It gently urged me forward when I was indecisive or confused—*Go here, not there. Do this, not that.* It was openhearted, strong, and very kind. Whether or not I listened, it always turned out to be right, and an agent for the highest good. The training gave that intuitive voice validity, and I will always be grateful to EST for reviving and empowering that part of me.

The impact on my life was immediate and profound. I helped set up an EST center in Newport Beach, and formed friendships that have lasted to this day. With new tools in hand, I dug even deeper, inhaling books on the impact of dominating mothers and absent fathers, and how to let go of inferiority and shame. I set out to heal old and festering wounds. By day, I was a dental receptionist, but at night, and in all my free time, I was a spiritual Amazon on a quest for wholeness.

I became my own driver, or so I thought. I was done with all those old patterns and dependencies, done with the outer-directed behaviors that led me to consistently doubt my own power and dim my own light.

Who needs a big strong man now, I thought?

Talk about setting myself up.

**That which I do not forgive in you,
lies unforgiven in myself.**

—Buddha

Dear reader, I couldn't move forward until I was able to *release the past*. I discovered that the two quickest routes to releasing the past are forgiveness and gratitude. Any spiritual path is ours to discover, and whatever road leads to that truth, ours to take. I'm so grateful I found a path that encouraged both forgiveness and gratitude.

I'm curious to know your experience with past hurts and resentments? What is your process for letting them go?

When we forgive ourselves, and others who have harmed us, we liberate ourselves for love. Forgiveness does not excuse the actions of others, but it does release us from poisoning ourselves with negative energy. If we can learn to let go of resentment, and feel thankful for every bump along the way, no matter how painful, we can move mountains!

Without forgiveness and gratitude, we will never be free. Release the past. Release those who have hurt us. Love is waiting for us!

7

OUT OF THE FRYING PAN...

What you resist, persists.

—CARL JUNG

The more work I did on myself, the more I craved authenticity and personal accountability with every interaction. I was determined to be my own woman in every way. Learning how to verbalize my needs more clearly seemed the obvious next step.

Deeper, clearer communication—that's what the latest advanced EST course promised and that's what I wanted.

The communications workshop would take place at the Los Angeles Convention Center. According to the application, completion of the EST basic training was a prerequisite.

Good, I thought, as I filled out my application form. Everyone there has been to boot camp, like me. I'll be surrounded by like-minded warriors.

The course spanned four days—Thursday and Friday evening, plus all day, and long into the night, both Saturday and Sunday. EST advanced courses were famous for their arduous hours, so I wasn't surprised or deterred.

I drove up from Orange County on Thursday right after work. The workshop started at 7:00. Promptness was not just a virtue for EST attendees, but a vow, and I sweated every clogged moment on the freeway. By the time I reached the Convention Center auditorium most of the two hundred and fifty attendants were already crammed inside. We were a sea of eagerness, our faces shining with enthusiasm as we faced the front podium.

I found an empty seat at the end of a row of chairs to the left, towards the back of the room. As the program started with the usual words of welcome from our workshop leaders, I felt somebody's eyes on me, to my right and close behind me.

The feeling persisted. I turned my head slightly, and sure enough, there was a man, also in an end chair, pinning me with his gaze. He didn't smile. He didn't frown. He didn't react at all. He just stared and stared and stared. I'm sure a small part of me noted that he was attractive, but most of me thought, *How rude*. I shifted my attention to the speakers up front, but every once in a while I glanced back.

Yup. Still staring.

The first practice our trainers presented was the equivalent of a crash course in mindfulness. Everyone seated on the left side of the room, including me, was instructed to line up and slowly move in one direction. Those seated people on the right were told to line up and move the opposite way. Whenever we stopped, we were directed to reach out and shake hands, while introducing ourselves to the person across from us—"Hello, my name is..." "Hello, my name is ..."—

We were instructed to then watch our thoughts.

In other words, say our names, while also noticing what our minds were saying.

I found it very interesting. I don't know about anyone else, but I was hearing my mind offer such highly enlightened observations as: "Too tall." "Too short." "Weird hair." "Who in their right mind wears stripes and checks together?"

This continuous swarm of mosquito-like judgments rose and fell and rose again. But something else was also going on. As I slowly moved down the line one person at a time, I started to notice that Gazing Man wasn't following instructions. He wasn't moving, he was waiting, waiting until I reached a point close to him. Then he slipped into the row and stuck out his hand.

"Hello, my name is Kathy," I said.

"Hello. My name is Jerry," he answered with a sly smile. I took his hand and shook it, watching as my mind said, "Okay. Kinda creepy."

I don't know how he did it, but as I kept moving left, he kept popping up in front of me, every other person it seemed like, re-introducing himself. "Hello, my name is Jerry." "Hello, my name is Jerry." One time he'd smile, the next time, laugh.

My mind hardened. What was it with this guy? First he won't stop staring, and now he won't stop introducing himself.

Why wasn't he following the rules?

Obnoxious.

Rebellious.

What. A. Jerk.

When it came time to share about the process on a group level, I kept these comments private. But I grumbled inside about Jerry the Gazer the whole drive home.

Friday afternoon, after another full day's work, I dragged myself back up to Los Angeles, battling traffic the whole way. I was grateful that I didn't see Jerry for the entire evening.

So much for that!

I booked a hotel room near the Convention Center for the next two nights—the commute was making me crazy. I slept the sleep of the virtuous.

I walked into the conference room a little bit early Saturday morning and blinked in surprise. Our instructors had drastically shifted the configuration. Pairs of chairs now faced each other, set close together, really close, as if for intimate confrontation. My stomach tightened.

Then I saw Jerry, sitting by himself, center-left.

There's that creepy guy again. Definitely not going to sit there.

I crossed to a table by the wall and poured myself a glass of water. I saw a group of familiar girls standing in the doorway—acquaintances from earlier courses. Good. Maybe I could sit with one of them.

But my feet had something else in mind. They started to weave between the clustered pairs of empty chairs.

Don't, I thought. *Don't do it. No no no no no, Kathy.*

I moved through the sea of empty seats as if pulled by an invisible force.

"May I sit here?" I said to Jerry, my voice prim.

"Oh, please do," he answered, equally polite. I plopped down in the chair directly across from his, so close our knees were almost touching.

"So, Kathy. Where are you from?" Jerry asked.

"Newport Beach area."

"Really? I took you for a Valley Girl," he teased. As proved to be the case so often with Jerry, I didn't know whether to be flattered or insulted. I would soon learn that keeping people off-balance was a special talent of his, for good and for ill.

My turn. "How about you?"

He beamed. "Long Beach. We're practically neighbors."

Oh.

The leaders stepped on stage and Day Three commenced. First up was a question-and-answer format. One person would speak, as the other practiced intentional listening. Next we were to reverse roles. Then one of us would move on to another empty chair. We were expected to experience a multitude of intimate interactions with as many strangers as possible.

Jerry spoke first. I listened as mindfully as I could, given his bright blue eyes. Then it was my turn. He took in every word.

Time for one of us to leave.

"I'll move!" Jerry said, his voice bright.

He trotted over to an empty chair. But after another round, he slipped back into the chair across from me. Then he did it again. And again.

While the goody-two-shoes in me protested—what if we got in trouble?—the latent rebel who once played hooky did a little jig.

"You're not following the rules," I told him, the fourth time he plopped in front of me, grinning.

"I wrote the rule book," was his answer.

Did I mention that I've always liked bad boys? Yes, Jerry seemed a bit slick, but he was also magnetic, and utterly self-confident. He let a few personal clues slip. He owned his own very successful company in Huntington Beach. My ears perked up at that. Nothing attracted me more than successful entrepreneurs. I might not ever get to be one, but the next best thing was rubbing shoulders with them.

He liked good food. Good wine. Nice boats.

Me three.

Time flew. Finally the evening break came. Jerry leaned close.

"There's a boat show here at the convention center," he said. "Can I buy you dinner?"

An hour later, we were clambering over fiberglass decks and hulls, munching on hot dogs slathered in mustard. Maybe not the most romantic first date but certainly one of the more original.

After investigating our tenth gleaming yacht, I checked my watch. "Time to go," I said. "I want to freshen up before things get started."

He cocked his head. "You're gonna be la-ate," he sing-songed. "And you know what *that* means…"

I certainly did. All EST instructors were extremely strict about time—if you were tardy, even by one or two minutes, you had to take immediate, verbal responsibility. They were very big on accountability, and so was I. But this little excursion with Jerry had made me feel deliciously reckless.

"Don't care," I said, my voice breezy. "You go on ahead. I'll take my knocks."

I found the ladies' room and put on a fresh coat of makeup. I looked in the mirror. My eyes and cheeks were glowing. When I got to the session, sure enough, all the doors were already locked. After finding the hall monitor and taking full and contrite responsibility for my lateness, he unlocked a side door.

The room was eerily silent—two hundred and fifty people sat quietly with their eyes closed in meditation.

Two hundred and fifty people, and guess where the attendant sat me? Right next to Jerry.

I bit back a rush of hilarity. I couldn't wait for him to open his eyes.

When he did, they widened slightly, but that was it. He probably assumed I'd planned things this way.

The next process started immediately—eye-gazing. This ancient Hindu technique required that we stare into each other's eyes for ten solid minutes.

It may feel like a lifetime, they warned, but try to stick with it.

Jerry should be pretty good at this one. Lots of practice.

I raised my eyes to meet his. After a few minutes, something shifted deep inside.

It was as if my soul left my body, lifting up to hover over my left shoulder. My spirit linked to his in an electric rush. I was awash in love and connection so piercing it was like a full body orgasm.

I'd just met this man, but I had never felt anything as powerful, or as confusing.

"Time for a twenty-minute break," a voice interrupted, breaking the spell. I felt myself return to my body. Neither of us could move.

"Did you feel what I just felt?" I asked Jerry.

He nodded, still not ready to speak. Yes, he had felt the same thing.

I grabbed one of the course leaders and started babbling about out-of-body experiences and interconnection and universal love.

He patted my arm. "Yes, yes. It's perfectly normal and natural with gazing. It happens all the time if you create the space for it."

But I didn't believe him. This was too special. We were too special.

Jerry and I moved to the far wall, talking, talking. Suddenly I couldn't get enough of this man. This was destiny—he was someone I was meant to know.

I wasn't even that surprised when Jerry confessed he hadn't actually taken the required basic EST course.

After all, he wrote the rulebook.

"Okay," Jerry said, long after midnight came and went. "I'm heading back home. Let's have breakfast at eight."

We'll see, I thought. He has a long round trip ahead of him.

At seven o'clock the next morning, my hotel phone rang. I was bleary-eyed, wrapped in the hotel bathrobe, my hair still in curlers.

"I'm down in the lobby," the already-familiar voice said.

"Come on up," I laughed, inviting him into my room, and my life, without a second thought.

I applied my make-up in the bathroom, my armor for the day. But this time Jerry watched, smiling, as he sat cross-legged on the floor, leaning against the tile wall. He chatted, his smile easy and comfortable, as if he and I had known each other for a hundred years.

I turned away from the mirror and met his eyes.

"Who are you?" I asked.

He stuck out his hand. "Hello," he said. "My name is Jerry."

I thought I had left behind the lovelorn little girl, but I was wrong. She was just waiting for her next moment. I linked my fate with Jerry's almost instantly. It felt so right. He was nothing like my ex-husband. He was strong and motivated and successful. I'd never met anyone like him. I fell head over heels in love.

We both agreed we were soul mates for life. And what a life it would be. Jerry was king of the hill, and I would be the adoring queen on his arm. He loved how we looked together. I felt like we'd been lovers for lifetimes.

So many green lights. So many red flags.

Any man who believes he wrote the rulebook is a man with utter self-confidence, but little humility. Charisma doesn't often translate into sensitivity. Jerry was dominating, wealthy, a force of nature. Yes, he swept me off my feet, but he used the same broom to sweep aside any part of me that didn't match his version of things. He urged me to change, but only in the direction to which he was pointing.

Jerry and I were together on and off for the next thirteen years. We never married, or lived together, but he was a partner, as well as a catalyst. I loved him so much. I chose not to notice other things—how sometimes control will wear the mask of encouragement. In time I changed jobs, and made more money. I felt strong and powerful at work, ten feet tall. But then I would join Jerry in the evening and shrink so that he could be tall.

Jerry needed so much oxygen! He'd take me to elegant restaurants and order us the most expensive food and wine on the menu. Then he'd be rude to the waiter, and I'd lower my eyes and look away. He claimed to be captivated by my spirituality and open-heartedness, but he considered them to be hobbies of mine, not my lifeblood. Mostly he was all business, and his business was all-Jerry, all the time. He was magnetic and larger than life, and I was so ready to be dazzled and wooed, I forgot who I really was.

Until Jerry himself reminded me.

Put down the weight of your aloneness and ease into the conversation. The kettle is singing even as it pours you a drink, the cooking pots have left their arrogant aloofness and seen the good in you at last. All the birds and creatures of the world are unutterably themselves. Everything is waiting for you.

—David Whyte

Dear reader, even now I long to reach back and comfort that needy girl—comfort any woman caught in an unhealthy place because of unhealed wounds—with these words—*trust in the process*. To say, like the Persian poet Hafiz, "I wish I could show you, when you are lonely or in darkness, the astounding light of your own being."

And yet. And yet. Other things, dear reader, are also true—We are where we are for a reason. We meet the people we're supposed to meet. And it takes what it takes for us to change. Everything we do is a stepping-stone to what happens next. Once you take that step, don't spend time and energy questioning it, just trust that you are once again standing in exactly the right place for you.

Hafez had something to say about this, as well: "The place where you are right now, God circled on a map for you."

When I met Jerry, some part of me still believed I needed a man to fix me, complete me. And the truth is, who I was back then still did. God circled Jerry on my map, and I will always be grateful. For Jerry proved to be an incredible gift, my springboard to unimaginable success.

Who has God circled for you?

8

CLIMBING THE LADDER

**There exist limitless opportunities
in every industry.**

**Where there is an open mind,
there will always be a frontier.**

—CHARLES KETTERING

Spending every day stapled to the front desk of a dental practice, phone glued to my ear, was a far cry from my airline stewardess fantasy. No cute uniforms for me in my twenties. No global adventures, no exotic locales. But at least my son Leo could come by after school and do his homework in the reception area as I filed patient information and answered the phone. At least I could pay our bills.

The gulf between the daily grind as a working mother and my nightly exploration of life's limitless potential widened with every month that passed. Leaving my husband for good was a first attempt to narrow that gap, even as I second-guessed myself. The EST course came next, a lifeline spanning drudgery and possibility.

I opened my mind to the idea of becoming more, just a crack. But a crack is sometimes enough.

One day, a colleague confronted me. She'd come to the dental practice to set up a new computer system, and I was put in charge of overseeing the installation.

"Kathy, you know you're way overqualified for this job, don't you?" she asked.

My cheeks flushed. A part of me knew she was right, but another part was unsettled by her comment. Yes, I was smarter than my work required, but that also meant I never felt dumb. Coasting might be boring, but it was also relaxing. I could do this job in my sleep, and when I went home, I left my work behind.

On the other hand, tackling a complex computer installation, working with data in a new way, exploring the parameters of online information all proved to be an exhilarating challenge. I'd forgotten this Kathy still existed—eager to learn, quick to adapt.

"Have you ever considered becoming a realtor?" she went on. "My husband runs a real estate company near here. You'd be great at it."

Like a kiss from a prince, her suggestion woke up my dormant ambition.

Getting a real estate license is no joke. It's like learning a new language—part business, part law, with a healthy dose of ethics on the side. Soon I was hacking my way through a thick jungle of deeds of trust, chattel mortgages, legal provisions and appraisals.

Words like *fiduciary* and *encumbrance* elbowed their way past *mouth guard* and *root canal* and I waved goodbye without a second thought.

The scariest, most exhilarating word for me? *Commission.*

I hadn't felt this motivated in years. I wouldn't get paid, unless I produced. The bigger the sale, the higher the reward. How great was that?

Selling real estate required an ability to understand a client's needs and communicate solutions clearly. You were part therapist, part economist—the job fit me like a glove. Soon I was regularly making four figures per commission. For the first time, I was financially comfortable. I was my own boss, and I loved that, too.

I can't overemphasize how much financial security meant to me. To be paid well was to be valued, and my self-confidence soared. I hadn't yet learned the distinction between self-confidence and belief in myself—the former comes and goes, while the latter never wavers— but this early taste of self-reliance was heady and encouraging. I might be dating a successful man, but my career, too, was flourishing. I liked the feeling of parity.

I also liked dressing up for work—and I don't mean those frumpy blouses with faux ties, boxy suits, and stodgy pumps that were considered appropriate wear for working women at the time. I filled my closet with soft jersey dresses in jeweled tones, purple, sapphire blue, gold. I wore stiletto heels and buttery leather jackets. I broke out of my chrysalis with richly embroidered wings.

Leo was eleven and growing tall and strong before my eyes. We had somehow survived the intense early years of struggle-and-juggle. True, he needed more of everything—more food, more clothes, more space—but I was able to provide more, too. I moved us into a three bedroom beachfront apartment back in Huntington Beach. The ocean sparkled outside our windows. The horizon lay beyond like a promise.

That said, there was still a strong divide between my two universes of success and spirituality. One delivered financial security, the other fed my soul, and never the twain should meet.

One day I was working hard on a particularly tricky escrow when I happened to glance at the realtor sitting at the adjacent desk—a sweet Asian gal. She was staring at the office door, her eyes wide with fear.

I soon discovered the cause. Just outside the glass entrance stood a priest, wearing the red robes of office and holding the biggest crucifix I'd ever seen. I knew our boss was a devout Catholic, but seriously? What was she thinking?

I touched my desk mate's arm.

"Look, I think I know what's about to happen here. Don't worry. You don't have to do anything you don't want to." Her shoulders lowered slightly.

Our boss called everyone together and told us the priest was here to bless her business. In a minute he was going to sprinkle holy water throughout our headquarters.

Not on my escrow papers, he isn't.

We stood in an awkward circle around him as he paused before each of us, proffering the giant crucifix. One by one, compliant realtors kissed the carved wooden feet and face of Christ.

"It's okay," I again whispered to my fellow resister. "Just put out your hand and say 'No thank you,' like this."

The cross soon reached me. I held up my palm. "No, thank you," I murmured, and the priest and crucifix moved on.

My office mate followed grateful suit.

I moved back to my desk and hastily tucked my papers safely away. Frankly, I was horrified. I couldn't imagine allowing personal beliefs to breach the wall of professionalism like this.

Over my dead body.

While I was buying and selling real estate, Jerry's import-export company was growing tentacles faster than any octopus.

One of his more successful product lines was alkaline batteries. Jerry's main supplier was Fuji Electrochemical, including their highly profitable Novel (pronounced No-Vell) brand. Jerry's company sold the Fuji Novel industrial batteries in bulk to medical and other facilities nationwide. Jerry credited his long term, successful relationship with Fuji on his understanding and ability to maintain "face" with his Japanese colleagues, a subject he loved to dissect and expound upon.

In 1983, five years after I took up real estate, the powers-that-be at Fuji set their sights on a new market. Duracell had recently come up with an innovative way of packaging for the consumer market—the blister card. Blister cards were the definition of user-friendly—the protective but transparent plastic window and compact size made products safe to ship, convenient to display, and best of all, easy to buy. The potential for individual store sales was huge.

Fuji told Jerry they wanted to break into the retail market by selling their alkaline batteries in blister packs. They asked Jerry to take the reins.

Jerry brought it up to me over dinner one night.

"Getting into retail is the last thing I want to do," he said.

"So, you'll turn them down?"

"I can't. If I do that, I'll lose face."

He smiled. I waited. I could tell he'd already worked out a solution.

"I'm going to tell them I accept their offer, but only if they give me an exclusive for the entire country. They'll never agree to that. It's my way out."

Fuji agreed to give Jerry the whole country.

Jerry called in a panic. "You have to help me, Kathy," he said. "You have to take on the retail side of my Fuji account."

I explained to him that I had at least thirty open escrows, with several more on the horizon. "Anyway, I don't know a thing about retail sales," I said.

"Sure you do. You're a natural," Jerry replied. "All you have to do is switch from talking about real estate to talking about batteries. We can work on this together. We'll identify the major chains and you can approach them"

"I'm sorry. I'm just too busy," I said.

"Kath," Jerry said, "please. I need you."

He needs me.

So I agreed, not because I wanted to, but because he needed me to.

I learned everything Fuji sent me—more about alkaline batteries than I ever wanted to know. I threw myself into this new endeavor. I would make sure the Fuji Novel brand was on every battery display case in every retail store nationwide.

My first cold call was to Lucky Markets, and Jerry was right, I *was* well suited to this new marketplace. Lucky signed on then and there, ordering blister cards for all 272 stores. I was ecstatic. I promised delivery within thirty days.

"Just one small issue," they said, as we shook hands on the deal. "We hate the name Novel—sounds too much like that Christmas carol. You know the one, The First Noel? We need you to change the name."

So now I had a massive order, but I didn't have a name. That meant I also had a truckload of blister card sleeves that no longer worked.

Back to the drawing boards. Jerry and Fuji batted around a bunch of ideas, and eventually landed on Fuji ElectroCell—battery-like, but without the tinsel.

Ninety days later, Lucky had their new product in every store. Fuji ElectroCell batteries proved to be big sellers and highly profitable for Lucky Markets. And I found out I loved the supply side of manufacturing.

I might still be selling Fuji batteries, were it not for one major drawback. My boyfriend was now also my employer. As long as I was scrambling to learn, and needed him to teach me, everything was fine. But as soon as I felt ready to take the reins, he had a hard time letting go. He wanted me to help him, sure, but he didn't want me to *replace* him. His need to maintain control kept pace with my desire to be independent, a race neither of us could win. Most of all, I didn't want to depend on Jerry for my income, as good as that income might be.

My intuitive voice kept whispering what I already knew. Working for Jerry was a bad idea.

If I stayed where I was, our relationship might not survive.

**Whatever you can do or dream you can do, begin it.
Boldness has genius, power and magic in it. Begin it now.**

—JOHANN WOLFGANG GOETHE

Dear reader, what is our truth? Are we making decisions on our own behalf, or someone else's? Can we learn to *clarify our intentions?*

I wasn't always willing to check my motives, but until I did, I couldn't stand in my own truth.

So many of us—especially women—have been trained to put the needs of others first, whether at home or at work. But sometimes it helps to ask this simple but powerful question before making a big change: Is this my dream, or someone else's?

We can't expect others to support our dreams if we haven't voiced them to ourselves.

Have you ever had to ask yourself the hard questions? Clear communication is scary, especially when it means verbalizing personal or professional needs or ambitions. Girls are neither taught nor encouraged to express 'demands'—the word itself takes on a different cultural tonality when referring to women. But clear expectations are both empowering and an effective tool of success. Not only that, doing what seems like the right thing for the wrong reason can backfire, a lesson I've had to learn the hard way. The truth is, we don't have to sell out our souls in the process of building a career!

Let's start by having an honest and intimate conversation with ourselves.

9

THE SKIRT IN THE ROOM

**Every great difficulty bears in itself its own
solution. It forces us to change our
thinking in order to find it.**

—NIELS BOHR

Jerry wasn't thrilled, but I was adamant. The time had come for me to secure a new job and a new boss.

I soon had a promising prospect, a sales and distribution company owned by five guys. It was basically a small, mom-and-pop—or in this case pop-and-pop-and-pop-and-pop-and-pop—packaging supply business with a warehouse based in the City of Commerce in Los Angeles. Their all-male sales force covered a limited but lucrative territory, distributing paper and plastic products to small local establishments.

Now the Five Guys were looking to expand.

They'd just set up a new division, Westcom, and created an exclusive sales position within it. This contract employee would be responsible for landing accounts with major retail chains nationwide—chains like Lucky Stores.

I was the only woman to apply for the position. The competition was fierce, and it was finally between me, and the last male applicant standing. After several interviews, I won the job. I was only half-surprised. After all, only one of the Five Guys would directly oversee the winner. His name?

Jerry.

Bye-bye batteries, hello packaging.

We set up shop in Tustin, Orange County. Westcom would pay me $1,500.00 a month for three months, and then I was on my own, paid only by commission. The cut in pay was dramatic, but my renewed independence felt priceless. I rapidly expanded my professional vocabulary to include terms like *corrugated cardboard* and *t-shirt bags*.

Boss Jerry and I shared an office, if you could call it that. My workstation was a small kitchen table located in the cramped anteroom, right across from Jerry's enormous desk. I had a single metal two-drawer filing cabinet, and one phone. Below me, orange shag carpeting. Above me, cottage cheese ceilings. Around me, beige walls—not a window in sight.

My stated mission was to snag large national chain stores, and leave the Southern California territories to the original sales force. But soon I also started cold calling and landing accounts with local enterprises, from catering businesses to retail grocery chains. As I worked the phones, the two drawers of my metal cabinet fattened with new client files.

Straws? I had them. Plastic spoons? No problem.

The Los Angeles County Museum of Art (LACMA) needed a new design for their shopping bags—creative work, and lots of fun, but also time-consuming, with only an itty bitty commission on the other side.

Once or twice a week I drove forty-five minutes one-way to the company headquarters in Commerce, to submit my orders and process quotations.

And day followed day, followed day. My bank balance was nice and healthy. My spiritual account was more and more in the red. The split inside between soul and career widened.

I attended a weekend event featuring Shirley MacLaine at the Bonaventure Hotel, along with six hundred other like-minded souls. I listened, rapt, as she talked about captivating notions of life after death and multiple souls, tales filled with spirit and mystery. I drank in her insight and humor and bold ideas.

"Listen," she said, reading from her book. " 'In all of the cosmos, there is nothing more valuable than a single soul, and whatever that single soul accomplishes in lifetime after lifetime uplifts the rest of humanity forever. That's how important each one of us is!' "

Monday morning, I was still floating from the weekend. I made the mistake of describing the event to Boss Jerry, after he remarked on my post-seminar glow.

Jerry thanked me for giving him such a good laugh. Later, I overheard him sharing the joke with his four cohorts. That Kathy. What a flake!

Never again, I decided.

Once a month I would take my seat at the long conference table, surrounded by men. I was still the sole member on the sales force missing a Y chromosome. The female receptionist would close the doors on us, and we'd sit in silence as the president looked over the sales totals for the month. Then he would eyeball the room.

"Looks like Kathy has the highest sales totals. Again. How do you guys like getting beat out by a skirt?"

I'd sit there thinking, Wow. That approach may motivate the men, but it sure doesn't motivate me.

I didn't feel acknowledged, I felt demeaned. But I said nothing. He got one thing right—I was making a lot on commissions. Why rock the boat?

The president took me out to a one-on-one lunch. Silly me, I thought it was to congratulate me on how well I was doing.

"You know what your problem is, Kathy?" he asked, patting my hand as if I were a child. "You're too nice to your clients."

"Excuse me?" I answered. I couldn't believe the arrogance. Should I remind him I was by far the highest producer in the company?

"I mean, I know you're a woman and all, but trust me, it's a dog-eat-dog world out there. You gotta get them before they get you."

What could I say? That I believed in leading with love? That in all of the cosmos, nothing was more important than a single soul?

Yeah, right. That would go over well.

Nighttime was my time, and it restored me. As I voraciously read whatever I could find on reincarnation and past lives, I found myself wondering—Was I repeating past mistakes, or rehearsing for a better future? Did reincarnation explain this intense inner conviction that I was meant for something different, something more?

But my resolve to keep my professional and spiritual world separate didn't waver, and I stayed silent on anything remotely esoteric at work. Why invite more laughter, more scorn? Until one day, the line between soul and striving not only blurred, it dissolved altogether.

He was a new client, an experienced buyer servicing the multiple eateries located at the sprawling, historic Los Angeles Farmers Market. With over one hundred vendors providing a daily flood of customers with delicacies ranging from Mediterranean platters to barbecued ribs, the Farmer's Market was an exciting challenge—talk about a broad range of packaging needs! I arrived at his office armed with stacks of information on paper and plastic goods. We got right to it. As he questioned me about to-go containers and disposable dinnerware, I rifled through the portfolio balanced on my lap, checking samples and quotes.

I'd been there maybe ten minutes when his voice grew quiet, almost tentative. "I would like to change the subject for a moment, please."

I paused, eyes aimed at an opened price list resting on my knees.

"I would like you to tell me everything you know about reincarnation."

Reincarnation? I stared at my lap, my heart pounding. He was my client. I was a professional. This was my worst nightmare. I flashed back to my real estate manager forcing everyone to kiss the cross. How mortifying.

When I finally looked up, embarrassment scalded my cheeks.

"Oh, I can see I've made you uncomfortable. I'm so sorry," he said. "But my three-month-old baby just died. This may sound strange, but somehow I believe you have something to teach me, something that I need to know."

My heart opened wide, and soon I couldn't believe the words pouring out of me. I shared everything I had been reading and learning about reincarnation. I talked about Shirley MacLaine, and Buddhism, and psychological research on the notion of past lives. As the conversation deepened and widened, I felt for him, and I felt *with* him.

This was no longer a sales meeting, but a meeting of souls.

But as soon as I left his office, I was filled with doubt, and overcome with a familiar shame. I had made such a point of closely guarding my spirituality at work, making sure never the twain should meet. How did he know?

I was caught with my spiritual slip showing, and I hated it.

Then another voice, wiser and kinder, whispered a different message. *Maybe there's no place to hide in the universe, Kathy. Maybe this client came to you by divine design.*

I tucked that possibility firmly away, put the walls back up and my head back down during office hours.

I'm a complainer by nature. Ask anyone who knows me—I don't withhold when something is bothering me. Boyfriend Jerry was getting a nightly earful about my job, and I was starting to drive us both crazy with my growing list of grievances.

Not that I considered leaving The Five Guys, no way! The money was already good, and I had just landed a new account that I suspected would become the goose that laid the biggest golden egg of all.

I was having Sunday brunch at my neighbor's house, when she mentioned a new building supply store she'd just visited in Huntington Beach. "They look like they could use a lot of your packaging supplies," she said.

My ears perked up. I lived in Huntington Harbor, so the store was literally down the street.

"You should definitely check them out," she urged.

So I did.

The Home Depot store was massive. As I moved from aisle to aisle looking for a new hose nozzle, I visually estimated over fifty thousand products—everything a homeowner would ever want or need. I found the perfect sprayer and got in line.

It soon became clear what my friend was talking about. "Packaging" was a generous term for the Home Depot procedure. At the end of every checkout stand someone had piled a huge stack of paper bags— like you'd get at the grocery store, only bigger. Each cashier would reach behind and grab a bag from the top of a pile sitting on the floor, a floor covered in grime and sawdust.

When I reached the front of the line, the cashier plucked a dusty bag from the stack. He gave it three or four shakes and dropped my sprayer into a paper sack big enough to hold a lawn mower. Then he carefully folded and refolded the top of the bag to reduce the unwieldy volume.

Not only was the set-up unsanitary, the process was ridiculously time-consuming.

My mind raced with ideas. I could save them so much time and money! As soon as I got home, I did some research, and quickly learned about the two enterprising entrepreneurs who founded this budding franchise. They were the real deal. They had both been fired from a major building supplies chain based in Southern California, and told they would never make it in the hardware business. Rather than folding up their tent, they took this as a challenge. They regrouped, and used their hard-earned experience to come up with a brand new vision; a building supplies company like no other. They called it the Home Depot. There were already three Depot stores locally—in Long Beach, Upland, and Huntington Beach—and twenty-five in total. The business model was unique and impressive, and the owners were looking to expand nationwide.

I made a cold call to the store supply center at their corporate headquarters in Atlanta. I might know nothing about drill bits and carpet tacks, but I knew I could save them a truckload of money when it came to packaging their products for customers. If they grew as fast as I suspected they would, Home Depot was going to want what I had to offer.

I was intrigued to learn that their buyer for expense products was female. Jane proved hard to track down—she had no designated office and was constantly flying from store to store and state to state. We traded cross-country messages before finally connecting a few days later. Like me, Jane was pleasantly surprised that I was a woman—the hardware world didn't attract a lot of females back then. But while my gender may have piqued her interest, it was my promise of storewide savings that held it.

I described the economic and hygienic advantages of t-shirt bags, and the convenience of smaller sacks for individual sales that could pop-up like Kleenex from individual dispensers.

"Oh, we looked into plastic at one point," Jane said. "But we were told it costs much more."

"No, no, no," I answered. "The paper guys are selling you a song. I can save you a lot of money."

She asked me to put together numbers on six packaging products, from t-shirt bags to twine. "Send your quotes to the Houston store," she added. "I'll let them know it's coming. I'll be there next week."

Now I had a dilemma. I needed to get quotes from our manufacturers, which meant bringing my boss into the loop. I knew Jerry wouldn't be thrilled at a new client with only twenty-five stores.

"Jerry? I have a new prospect," I said.

Jerry glanced up from his desk.

"It's a building supplies chain called Home Depot. They're based out of Atlanta and…"

"How many stores?" he interrupted.

"Well, twenty-five for now, but…"

Jerry threw both hands in the air. "Forget about it," he said.

As usual, all Jerry cared about was the current store count of the client, not the future possibilities. Usually I backed down, but not today. I leaned across my kitchen-table desk, my voice steely.

"No," I said. "I don't want to forget about it. The two guys that started Home Depot? They're on a mission. It may be small now, but it's going to grow into a major, major retailer. I know I'm right about this."

Jerry's eyes narrowed, as if deciding whether or not to put up a fight. Finally, he shrugged. "Fine," he said. "You want to pursue this, go ahead. But you're on your own, understand?"

I called around for the best prices and mailed off quotations on six initial packaging products to the Houston Home Depot. I wasn't sure Jane would even get the list, much less respond to it. I could picture it getting lost in the shuffle.

But she called within days.

"This all looks pretty good. I'm coming to Southern California in a few weeks," Jane said. "Where shall we meet?"

I eyed the orange carpeting, shaggy as a sheepdog. The chipped Formica table. The windowless walls. And Jerry, sitting a few feet away.

"I'll come to you," I said.

My boss Jerry often accompanied me on big client calls—to help with call spreads, he said. But I suspected it was also to make sure he could do his man-splaining thing if necessary. This time I'd be on my own, negotiating woman-to-woman. I couldn't wait.

Jane and I met at the Long Beach store.

"Your quotes are very competitive," she said. And we started down the list.

I again mentioned dispenser boxes, so that cashiers could more easily retrieve individual bags.

"Won't that be more expensive?"

"Just the opposite," I said, and followed up with numbers and facts.

We moved on to T-shirt bags for medium-sized items, which could hang from a metal brace at arm's reach.

"Can you install and demonstrate the new system?"

"Absolutely," I fibbed.

I kept offering products, and she kept saying yes. We hammered out prices that were fair to both sides, and not a single dog ate another dog.

"One last question," Jane said, as she signed the Purchase Order. "Can you get me truck seals?"

Truck seals?

"Sure. No problem," I answered, picturing a herd of barking sea mammals in the bed of a pick-up. "I'll get back to you with a fair price." (For the record, truck seals are the plastic security locks used to seal off truck containers, to make sure nothing gets tampered with between the loading and unloading of product.)

Jane sat back, thinking. "Here's what I'd like to do," she said. "I won't lie to you—we're working with another manufacturer's rep who has comparable quotes as well. So I'm going to split up the country and give half to you, half to your competitor. How do you feel about taking on our seventeen stores in Florida?"

"I feel fine about it."

"It's going to be a challenge," she warned. "All the blue hairs live in Florida, and they do not like change. Let's see if you can make this new system work while keeping a lid on complaints. You'll also need to fly to Florida to help the stores transition to t-shirt bags. How about I meet you in Miami, and we'll see how it goes after that?"

Which is how I found myself in a sweltering Miami Home Depot side-by-side with Jane and my bag manufacturer rep Rick, drilling in screws for metal t-shirt bag racks. Unfortunately, Rick turned out to be old school, by which I mean a misogynistic jerk. As the three of us traversed Florida in a rental car, Rick started to drive Jane crazy. By the end of the first week of in-store installations, she was at her wit's end. I was in danger of losing the whole business.

I made a snap decision—to opt for the truth. I took her aside.

"Look. You know and I know Rick is a chauvinist pig," I said. "But I promise you, from now on you'll only do business with me. I'll handle everything, and you'll never have to deal with him again."

After that, I did it all—drilling, installing, loading, training. I did it all in Florida, I did it all in Texas, I did it all in Arizona.

Finally Jane conceded that I had won her over, and I got the whole country.

Within three years, twenty-five stores had become four hundred, with no end in sight. The Five Guys might not have wanted me to pursue the Home Depot account, but they had no problem at all depositing the steady influx of bigger and bigger checks. Jane sent more and more items for quotes, and orders grew exponentially. By now, she and I had become friends as well as colleagues. Compatibility and collaboration flavored every conversation. Trust set the tone, mutual success and profitability followed.

As an independent contractor, I was paid solely by commission—a third of whatever I brought in. No insurance benefits, no pension. Technically I was free to work for other companies as well, but I chose to put all my attention where I was. The Home Depot account kept expanding, and I was making hundreds of thousands of dollars… for the Five Guys.

Boss Jerry was ecstatic. Boyfriend Jerry was livid, and he let me know it.

One memorable occasion, we met for a quick lunch at a local restaurant. I don't remember what we ordered, but the meal was spiced with my usual heated complaints about work.

Jerry pushed his plate away, his food barely touched.

"Are you okay?" I asked.

"No, I'm not! I feel like a broken record," he said. "Kathy, you don't need them. They. Need. You."

This discussion always wound up in the same cul de sac, or should I say dead end. Jerry would tell me I should leave. I would insist I couldn't. Neither of us would budge.

"Quit," Jerry said to me, as we finished our meal. "Find a job you love."

"That's easy for you to say," I flung back. "You work for yourself."

"So work for yourself. Start your own company!"

"I can't," I said, my heart beating harder. "You know I can't. Home Depot is *my* client. I've been with them from the start. They rely on me."

Jerry stood up. "I am so tired of you refusing to honor yourself and your abilities. When is this going to stop? When are you going to break away, stand on your own two feet? I can see how talented you are. *Why can't you?*" His eyes filled with tears. I was astonished. I had never seen him cry.

He grabbed the check and left.

I sat at the table for a long time. I knew Jerry was right. I did have to make a change. But even small tectonic shifts lead to repercussions. This would be a massive change, an earthquake in my life.

Not now, I thought. Not yet.

**Each person is born with an unencumbered spot, free of
expectation and regret, free of ambition and embarrassment,
free of fear and worry; an umbilical spot of grace
where we were each first touched by God.
It is this spot of grace that issues peace.**

—MARK NEPO

Dear reader, oh, how I long to shout this from the rooftops! *Never stay for
the money.* I know, I know, easier said than done. I held on far too long, and
more than once. Each time, I thought I couldn't leave a job, because I was
making a good income. But trust me, the price tag is too high. The longer we
stay where we do not belong, simply because we fear financial insecurity,
the harder it is on our souls, not to mention our bodies.

As Bruce Lipton writes, "Most illness is just stress from not living in
harmony." We are a culture suffering more and more from depression,
stress-related illnesses, and general malaise, and moving up the ladder does
not make us immune. If you wake up in a state of dread and drag yourself
to work, pay attention to what your soul is trying to tell you!

What happens when we sell ourselves short day after day? When our
environment doesn't support us, doesn't recognize, much less embrace the
dearest part of our heart? What happens when we try to fuel our growth
using an obsolete energy source, like a rusted battery that has outlived
its usefulness?

I'll tell you what happens.

We suffer.

We can choose to ignore it—the pain of knowing we're not where we
should be, that we are out of alignment with our true purpose. But we turn
away from this deep ache at our own peril. Because after a while, we grow
numb—forget that change is even possible.

Or...

We can open our eyes wider. Pay attention to the pain. Because it is
in those darkest of moments, when we're caught on our own crucible of
discomfort, that signals from Spirit appear. Like lanterns of light, they guide
us toward our truer selves.

At least that has been my experience. Has it been yours?

10

THE WRITING ON THE WALL

**Everyone has been made for some particular
work, and the desire for that work has
been put in every heart.**

—JALALUDDIN RUMI

I blame Rosie's painting for my dark night of the soul.

Boyfriend Jerry and I were flying to Sedona with our friend Wes for a little getaway. The steady drone of the airplane was soothing, and my eyelids drooped. Outside the window, flat clouds hovered over an ochre landscape, dusty and dry. Jerry had taken the middle seat. Wes sat by the aisle.

I rested my head against Jerry's shoulder. "I can't keep my eyes open," I said. "Work this week was exhausting."

"That's what happens when you're not where you're supposed to be. If you had your own company…"

"Jerry, don't start," I said, my voice tight. "We're on vacation, okay? Give it a rest."

He unbuckled his seat belt with a snap and jumped to his feet.

"Where are you going?"

"Don't worry, I'll be right back," he said. "I'm just going to go to the front of the plane. And I'm going to tell everyone, seat by seat, that you will work for them and they can keep two-thirds of the profit. And then I'm going to see how many takers we have."

I pulled on Jerry's sleeve. "Sit down," I said. "Just stop already, will you?"

He plopped back down. "What you're doing right now? The amount of money you're making for your bosses? It's insane."

I turned away, pressing my forehead against the chilled glass. I didn't want to think about work. I wanted to think about our workshop with Lucretia in Sedona. I was officially off the clock.

Lucretia was a spiritual teacher and channeler—part of my "other" world, the one outside of my cramped office in Tustin. Her event would include group gatherings and personal sessions, for twenty or so eager students. I was especially hoping to receive some personal guidance from Abdullah, an ancient entity who spoke through Lucretia.

As we found our seats in the meeting room, I noticed an easel set up on one side of the dais. A blank canvas rested on the easel, along with numerous brushes and small pots of paint.

Lucretia stepped up front.

"I want to introduce a very dear friend to you," she said. "Her name is Rosie, and she is a special kind of artist. She's a painter of souls, or rather the soul's purpose for being here."

A shiver climbed up my spine. I might not understand the terminology, but I resonated with the concept.

A short, stocky woman joined Lucretia, her gentle face capped with a soft crown of graying hair. She waited, wrapped in shy silence, as Lucretia explained further.

"Rosie was in college the first time it happened. She was painting a landscape in art class, when suddenly it felt as if someone else was moving her hands. She was no longer a painter, she was a conduit.

Something needed to be created, and Spirit required her hands to do the manifesting."

I couldn't put this powerful concept together with the sweet, unobtrusive woman before me. Really?

Rosie stepped in front of the easel. Lucretia told us that today Rosie would be painting the soul of a man sitting in the audience—she'd asked his permission before the seminar began, and he was more than willing to give it.

Jerry leaned forward in his seat. He was as fascinated as I was.

Rosie closed her eyes and grew still. The room settled with her, restlessness smoothing into deep silence.

Rosie's hands began to dance across the blank canvas, as if of their own accord. The brushes flew so fast I could barely keep track. Dab, dab, dab, dab. White here, blue there, then red, then white again. The features of a woman emerged as if surfacing from underwater, appearing in the middle right hand corner.

"Look," I whispered to Jerry. "She's so beautiful."

But even as I spoke Rosie was at it again, more daubs of paint, across the top, moving downward, then swatches and sweeps and the face was gone, covered by swirls of color and light.

"Why'd she paint over the woman's face?" I again whispered.

Jerry shrugged, his eyes glued on Rosie's dancing hands.

Within twenty minutes, the painting was complete, the canvas fully covered.

Rosie seemed to shake herself awake. She looked over at Lucretia and nodded.

Lucretia turned to us. "It is finished," she said.

I cornered Rosie during the break. "Why did you cover that woman's face in paint?" I asked.

She smiled. "I don't remember."

I must have looked puzzled.

"No," she said, "I mean, I don't remember doing that. Any of it. I'm not really painting, you see. It's more like… listening. Spirit moves my hands and chooses the colors." She glanced across the room at the painting, still resting on the easel. "If there's an image of a woman, it will appear when the person is ready to see it. Spirit paints in layers. That's why, when I hear 'it is finished,' I put down the brush and never touch the painting again. The lessons emerge in their own time."

Rosie's process was threefold. First, she entered a kind of preparatory trance. While in this deep awareness, she would ask about her subject's soul. The answer came in the form of automatic writing, a stream of consciousness from pen to paper, not of her own accord. Next was the act of painting itself, also guided, also automatic. Finally, when all the paint had dried, Rosie would once more go into a deep meditative state, and ask for the meaning of the painted images she had no memory of creating. She would orally record these impressions. Ultimately, her clients received the writing, the painting, and a tape recording describing the myriad meanings hidden within the work.

Jerry was very, very excited about getting this done. I wasn't so sure—what if Spirit took a closer look at me and didn't like what she "saw"? What if Jerry was right, and my soul wasn't shaping up the way the universe wanted?

My personal reading with Lucretia later that day only exacerbated my worries. Lucretia, too, received directives from entities in the Spirit world, which she would then pass along to her clients. One was called Abdullah, but he might as well have been called Jerry, given his message to me.

"I see your name on three different corporations," Abdullah intoned.

I stiffened in my seat.

"What do you think about that?" he pressed, after it became clear I wasn't about to respond, not without prompting.

"It sounds like a lot of work," I said.

"Oh, no, my dear," Abdullah answered, his voice amused. "It sounds like a lot of power. You have a great mind. It would be a shame to waste it."

Humpf.

Jerry decided to throw a party on his yacht, with Rosie as his featured guest. She would manifest a painting of his soul's purpose while our friends watched—a floating showcase of her special talent.

Daubing trance-inspired paint on an easel while keeping balance on a yawing yacht was quite a challenge, but somehow Rosie managed. (She did admit she'd never do it again.)

Jerry's soul painting was bold and crammed full of vibrant images. A spill of exotic Asian lettering tumbled down the left hand side. I was tempted to label the characters Japanese, what with Jerry's Fuji connection and all, but who knows what ancient Asian pictographs Rosie was channeling?

"Every two thousand years an entity like this one comes through," began the accompanying message, before launching into a recitation of past lives replete with warrior kings and conquerors. As Rosie put it later, "Wow. Jerry is one powerful soul." She didn't have to tell me. I already knew.

I couldn't wait to have my own soul painting done. I found out I didn't even have to be in the same room—all she needed was my permission.

Rosie was in Palm Springs at the time. As soon as she was finished depicting my soul's purpose, she ferried the painting directly to my house, wrapped in brown paper and tied up with twine.

I called Jerry. "It's here."

"Don't look until I get there," he said. "Promise."

Jerry joined me on the living-room sofa for the unveiling. As Rosie unwrapped the paper covering, my heart fluttered. I couldn't wait to see what my soul had to say.

"It's so interesting," Rosie commented, as she tipped the canvas our way. "This turned out to be the tallest figure I've ever painted."

A robe-shaped form, royal blue in color, dominated the canvas. The head area was framed in white light, but the actual face was kind of murky, and had no features. I made out what looked like a pair of humongous outspread wings, one on each side.

I couldn't help myself. "Well, I always knew I was an angel," I quipped.

Rosie shook her head. "No, no, no, dear. Those aren't wings. When I asked, I was told they are fountains of living water to feed the thirsty."

Yes. I could just decipher the outlines of kneeling figures on both sides of the canvas, all of them leaning in toward the central form.

Rosie went on, "I asked Spirit, 'Who would it be that thirst?' And the answer that came was 'For the most part, women. You will show women how to be soft, but also strong. How to stand on their own two feet and come into equal power with men. How to balance the male and female energies.'"

My thoughts tumbled and spun.

I'm supposed to help a bunch of those soft, fluffy women with whiny voices Oh, could you do this? Could you do that? So clingy and incapable and full of needs?

I stood up, my cheeks on fire. "No! If this is my life's path, I don't accept it. Where's the contract? Show me the small print so I can X it out, because no way am I doing this!"

I ran from Rosie, from Jerry, from the faceless Amazon with her spewing fountains and fragile cowering females. I threw myself on my bed and wailed into the pillow. Out in the living room, I could hear Jerry conferring with Rosie, his voice urgent.

Soon the mattress shifted as Rosie lowered onto the edge of the bed, her warm, solid weight a comfort. I turned toward her, face blotched, eyes streaming.

She studied me, a small frown furrowing her brow. Then her face cleared. "Oh, I see," she said. "You think that you have to go out and *do* something. What if I were to tell you, you just have to be the best

Kathy you know how to be? Just do that, and you have no idea how many women you're going to touch. You'll be helping by example."

The words provided a glimmer of hope. "Just be myself?"

"Just be yourself. The best Kathy."

"Well, I can do that," I said, sitting up.

I mean, wasn't I already spending every waking moment bettering myself, being my best, strongest, most independent and authentic self?

Every moment?

Well, not counting work, of course, where I had to keep a lid on things, but that was different.

Day and night?

Well, maybe not when I was with Jerry, and I made the choice to shrink, so he could be bigger, but let's face it, he needed to be the strong one.

Rosie touched my hand. "You have more power than you even know, dear. Spirit told me. You are surrounded by souls ready and willing to support you with this."

There was more, and my earlier suspicions about reincarnation proved well-founded. Apparently, this present path of mine was a kind of do-over, an opportunity to get it right. I had allegedly once been a Mesopotamian queen—ha!—but my reign had been petulant and indignant. I had put people to death on little more than a whim. Now the energy of the queen had reappeared.

"You have her strength and her abilities," Rosie explained, "but this time you chose to come on the ray of love."

"The ray of love. . ?"

She elaborated. Any time I became overly impatient—insisting on getting my way, stomp-stomp-stomping my feet—that response, rather than speeding things up, would act as a drag on everything.

"But if you stay centered. If you use the strength of the queen *and* the power of love, then you can be a great healing force for women everywhere."

Rosie was offering me a corridor to a new way of being. But I still wasn't sure I wanted to go down that hallway.

I had a complex relationship with members of my own sex. I was happy when my peers did well, but that joy was not always reciprocated, especially when a woman was insecure, and hadn't done her own inner work. It seemed as if I was reflecting back at them things they hadn't handled in their own lives. They didn't know what to do with me. They resented my perceived strength.

And I resented their perceived weakness.

The truth is, any resentment is usually a reflection of some resistance and lack we feel about ourselves. When someone presents a trait that personally challenges our own self-image, it triggers strong opposition in the form of jealousy, dislike, or judgment. The reaction occurs automatically, and often unconsciously. For women struggling with issues of powerlessness, a seemingly strong, confident female can evoke such reactivity. And women overly identified with power will reject insecurity.

I could always feel the former, probably because I grew up with this exact dynamic between my mother and me. I felt other women's dislike of me, of my success, felt it in the bones and sinews of my body. Their insecurity acted like an energy-drain.

Why on earth would I want to invite more of that neediness into my life? It sounded horrifically arduous.

You don't have to do anything. Just be the best Kathy you can be.

I hung the painting on the bedroom wall across from my bed, determined to go on with life as usual. But it haunted me, this portrait of my soul's purpose. Every day I would wake up, glance at the painting, and wonder, Where is my face? Why don't I have a face? As I zipped up my skirt and stepped into my high heels, I'd find myself gnawing on questions like a puppy with a chew toy—If my path is to shine like a beacon for other women, why do I continue to dim my own light?

If I'm to model the new feminine energy, what am I resisting? What am I not seeing for myself?

And most terrifying of all—If this is my life's purpose, what am I doing in an unbalanced relationship with Jerry?

You see, Rosie neglected to tell me I wasn't just a woman overflowing with living waters. I was also a woman dying of thirst.

Like a responsible patient, I sought out a second opinion, then a third and a fourth. But the spirit world was unanimous: The writing, like my painting, was on the wall. My destiny lay in integrating and strengthening masculine *and* feminine energy. The time had come to show up fully for my life.

As the painting poked more and more holes in my self-image, work became a constant tug-of-war between the entrenched values of a macho culture and my evolving ones. The Buddha put it best, "The cause of suffering is resistance to change." The harder I dug in my heels, the more I suffered. Finally, I couldn't tolerate the misalignment any longer. I had to make a change, no matter how scared I felt. Once again, the time had come to hold my feet to the fire. To trust in myself, and stake a claim on my future.

I needed to start my own company.

When inspired by a grand purpose, a wonderful project, your thoughts shatter their bonds, your mind travels beyond limitations; your consciousness extends in all directions; and you discover a new and amazing world. Hidden forces, talents and faculties spring to life and you find yourself to be far greater than you ever dreamed you could be.

—PATANJALI

Dear reader, are you struggling, as I was, to *find your soul's purpose*? If you are, and you're anything like me, I can even tell you where to look! As Joseph Campbell says, "The cave you fear to enter holds the treasures that you seek." Where in your life are you holding back? Where do you have the most fear around making a change? Is there an action you long to take, yet can't imagine taking?

Trust me, that way lies gold.

If we give in to fear, we will remain stuck. We may never know what we are truly here to do and be. If we become open and teachable, the right teachers will come.

Don't put this journey off, as I once did. On the introductory page of *A Course in Miracles* the opening statement concerning personal transformation says it best—"This is a course in miracles. It is a required course. Only the time you take it is voluntary." I think about this all the time, how change is inevitable and spiritual growth is mandatory. How, like it or not, the timetable for personal transformation is up to us.

Dear friend, realizing our true purpose is not a question of if, but when.

Why not now?

11

WELCOME TO THE FURNACE

Strive not to be a success,
but rather to be of value.

—ALBERT EINSTEIN

If I was going to have my own company, first I needed a name.

I believe in the power of language. Words matter. Before I did anything else, I spent weeks researching potential names and their meanings. I knew that above all, I wanted my company moniker to connote excellence, as well as trustworthiness. Over Christmas, I drove to the Orange County Courthouse in Santa Ana with a short list of candidates, to check on their availability.

My number one choice was Qualis. Qualis is the Latin root word meaning "a degree of excellence and quality." I loved that! I might need to change the *content* of my work, but I would never again compromise the *context*. Qualis perfectly reflected my desired context, one of excellence and integrity. I added 'International' because I didn't want to put limits on the future. It was a nod to the young Kathy parked in the fields near LAX, her eyes following glinting airplanes as they soared to faraway worlds.

The name was available! I filled out the necessary forms and paid a small fee. I would no longer be the skirt in the room. I would be Kathleen Gardarian, dba Qualis International.

"From now on," I told the president when I returned to work in January, "please make out all commission checks to Qualis International."

"What's Qualis International?"

"My new dba."

"You can't be serious," he said.

The president summoned me to the City of Industry headquarters. His secretary ushered me into the familiar conference room, and closed the door with a firm click. I faced the table. There they sat, all five guys, arms across their chests like tactical shields.

I took a chair directly across from them.

The president passed me a sheet of legalese with a space for my signature.

"We'd like you to sign where indicated, please."

I scanned the document. "I'm sorry," I said. "But what is this?"

I knew what it was. I just wanted him to say it out loud.

"It's a non-compete clause." The president's voice was stern. The other four matched his scowl. They were doing their best to intimidate.

I pushed the paper back his way. "You know what," I said, "I don't know what I am going to do with Qualis International but I sure as hell am *not* going to sign this and limit my options. And by the way? I'm an independent contractor. That means you have no right to ask me."

"But you're a woman," he said, genuinely surprised. "You can't own a company. What on earth makes you think you can run one?"

I walked out.

The non-compete fiasco was their first mistake. The second was to undermine me with my clients. The president called them one by one, promising the reps better deals, pressuring the buyers to circumvent me.

Perhaps if I had followed the president's early advice, to "be tough and get 'em before they get you," these tactics might have worked. But

I had established close and mutually respectful business relationships. Instead of betraying me, my clients sprang to my defense.

The calls poured in. "What's the deal with your employers?" they asked. "Why are they saying these things? You're our rep. We trust you."

"What the heck is going on out there, Kathy?" Jane said, on an emergency call from the Depot headquarters in Atlanta. "I want to work with you, not them."

If ever I needed proof of the power of integrity, here it was. The five guys' paradigm of dog-eat-dog had boomeranged, and badly.

On August 11, 1988, the City of Los Angeles stamped my official incorporation papers. Qualis International, Incorporated was legally born. I'd fulfilled my usual Westcom orders in July, but purposely cut back on production in August. My gut told me I wouldn't receive a penny more in commission the moment I left for good. A substantial July check arrived on August 15th. I made a beeline to the company bank in downtown Los Angeles and cashed it. I wasn't taking any chances. The night before, I had typed up a letter of resignation. I drove directly from the bank to FedEx and sent it overnight express.

The president called me first thing the next morning. "Kathy, this is terrible," he said. "We can't have you resign! You're too important to the company."

I listened, my anger growing. Suddenly I was the best thing that had ever happened to them. Whatever I wanted was mine for the asking. Promotion to a full-time position? No problem. President of the division? Just say the word and the new title was mine.

"It's not about titles!" I said. "It's about values. I need to be in a place where I feel empowered. Where I'm in a position to make a real contribution. Where who I am is appreciated."

I might as well have been speaking Egyptian.

Once my boss realized I was resolute about quitting, he quickly began implementing his professed 'work ethic.' He called every single manufacturer in town and told them not to give me quotes or sell products to me. He warned them that if I approached them, they shouldn't do business with me, or else.

But once again, his threats fell on deaf ears. With only one exception, my manufacturers, too, were not only happy but eager to keep working with me. (Only one established company on the East Coast couldn't bring themselves to sell to a new, woman-owned company. More on them later.)

I set out on my new path fueled by pure, Grade A anger.

Don't think a woman can run her own business? Watch me.

My intention was not only to do well, but to soundly beat the five guys at their own game. I would be the absolute best!

My perfectionism, never that far from the surface, rose to take the wheel.

I was still living in a two-bedroom condominium in a complex called the Broadmoor in Huntington Beach, a two-story, butter yellow building with a tile roof. Small individual balconies overlooked a private lagoon, with a distant view of Huntington Harbor. With Leo away at college, this became the headquarters for Qualis International. I dragged a heavy brown wooden desk into the bedroom, where it took up most of one wall. It was ugly and ungainly, but at least I finally *had* a desk. I set my Underwood typewriter on it—no computers yet for this enterprise. I parked a FAX machine on the dresser in the adjacent bedroom, once Leo's, now for guests.

Instead of orange shag, I padded around on beige industrial wall-to-wall carpeting. A small bedroom window let in the morning light, and my patio had a view of the marina harbor. I could just about hear waves slapping against boat hulls, and seagulls calling to each other, perched on wooden masts.

Naturally, Home Depot required a completely new set of quotes, now that contracts would be with Qualis International. The Five Guys submitted a fresh bid, as did a slew of other rep companies nationwide. They all had infrastructure, and corporate history, and massive manpower.

But I had me. I understood precisely where the Home Depot pricing had been, and therefore where it would now have to be to win a new bid. Yes, I was one woman working alone in my house, but that meant no overhead. I had much more leeway to price competitively.

I compiled a revised list of prices, and was ready to submit as soon as I received my final quote from the twine company I had always used while at Westcom. Then I hit a snag. Unbeknownst to me, the East Coast twine company rep had been stringing me along for weeks, no pun intended. At the last minute, he informed me they would no longer supply me with twine, they'd stick with the Five Guys.

I allowed myself five minutes of full-blown panic. Then I took a deep breath, and called my Home Depot buyer, Jane. I shared my dilemma. Almost four years of working together under an umbrella of mutual honesty and support made that call possible. Sure enough, she knew of another company, right in downtown Los Angeles.

"They manufacture a fine twine," she said. "As long as it's the same tensile strength, there's no reason you can't use them."

The clock was ticking. I drove straight to their Los Angeles factory and sat with their rep until we had worked out a fair and competitive price for their best spiral-twisted twine. I submitted the bid to Home Depot on a Friday afternoon, just under the wire.

By Monday, the Home Depot account was mine. My old boss was furious—at me, at the manufacturers, at the Depot. Honestly, I think he would have been okay with losing the account, as long as "the skirt" didn't win it.

I assumed landing Home Depot meant I'd crossed some sort of finish line, but it was only the first lap. Every day I dressed for work in the same room where I sat down at my desk. Along with skirts and heels, I was wearing a tall stack of hats: secretary, treasurer, buyer, seller, CEO, chief cook and bottle washer. There was nothing I didn't do, including the day-to-day bookkeeping—I literally kept a black leather book with me at all times, so I could track my products. I had columns of invoice numbers on dozens and dozens of inventory SKUs (Stock Keeping Units), paid and unpaid, delivered and pending.

I thought I was working alone. I soon realized I had company, a familiar, if uninvited guest. His name was Fear, and he'd returned to his favorite spot, just to my left, a tall, steely pillar, looming and immovable. He nipped at my confidence, kept pace with my success.

Are you sure you're cut out for this? Do you really know what you're doing?

I feel you, I said. I know you're there.

And…?

And nothing. I know you're there, but come on along. Because I'm doing this anyway!

My first order came in, not from the Depot, but from Cornet Stores. It was a twenty thousand dollar total bid, which meant I had to shell out ten thousand dollars up front to initiate the manufacturing order. I borrowed the money from my personal savings account and crossed my fingers. Within thirty days, my company was in the black.

Then Jane at Home Depot threw another curveball. Would I get a quotation from China for merchandise bags? She was hoping to cost-average our domestic orders by manufacturing and importing a portion from over there.

I had never worked with an international banker, much less been anywhere near China.

"Sure," I said, as Fear slowly wagged his head in disbelief.

China. Where to start?

I let intuition take the lead. A memory jiggled free, rose to the surface. What about those business acquaintances I once met in Vancouver? Didn't they have connections in China?

I made the call.

Sure enough, they knew of a trustworthy broker living in Hong Kong. Within weeks I had spoken to him. Yes, he had a suitable factory, located in the south of China. I booked a flight to Kai Tak International Airport in Hong Kong.

I spent much of the fourteen-hour journey poring over reams of information pertaining to international manufacturing codes, shipping containers and import fees. There was an empty seat to my left, and I piled it high with stacked folders.

We flew due west, crossing time zones and oceans in what felt like an eternal nighttime. Finally the sky began to lighten, and the pink glow of dawn illuminated the spectacular Hong Kong urban-scape.

Suddenly the wings canted sharply. I glimpsed a wide red-and-white checkered banner on a hillside as the pilot executed a steep 45° turn. The plane straightened out and threaded an impossibly low and narrow path right between the Hong Kong skyscrapers. If I'd wanted to, I could have peeked in a few windows and noted what the residents were having for breakfast. We landed on a runway half on land, half on sea. One skid, and we'd be underwater.

I wasn't afraid. I was elated. But not because I'd survived that hair-raising landing. No, I'd just realized something even more miraculous. The seat to my left wasn't only empty because no one had paid for it. It was empty because Fear had finally deserted his post. I was too busy working to be afraid, and that, apparently, was the key. Action is a powerful solvent. The steel pillar of terror had simply dissolved.

My broker greeted me outside Hong Kong customs, along with the owner of the bag-manufacturing factory. Soon all three of us were skimming across the South China Sea on a jetfoil boat, our destination the south coast of mainland China. Within an hour, I was sitting inside the factory, spreading out stenciled artwork for the custom plastic bags. One logo was the familiar Home Depot lettering. The other was for Qualis International.

These days merchandise bags are machine cut, but back then everything was done by hand. The workers were all local women, and they hand-cut a beautiful, sturdy product. We agreed on a first order—four shipping containers' worth of bags. Qualis International had earned its global badge of honor.

On to the next step of my learning curve. Home Depot wrote up an initial order for the four containers, two headed for the Port of Charleston, two for the Port of Los Angeles. Their payment would remain "on file," to be released, bank-to-bank, as soon as the contents of the containers were checked and cleared at the two ports. It was like a promise to pay, but someone on my end had to front the initial amount to kick-start the process of manufacturing. When your main client was a retail chain expanding as fast as the Home Depot, a personal savings account would no longer do. The situation required a substantial business Line of Credit.

I needed a willing bank, one that could provide maximum financial flexibility, no easy task for a new, woman-owned company. I reached out to my boyfriend Jerry—he loved nothing more than rescuing a damsel in distress! With one call he arranged an appointment with the bank manager he used for his own complex and expansive business endeavors. He agreed to meet me at the bank manager's office and personally make the introduction.

I called him from my car the next morning. He hadn't checked in to confirm, which was not like him.

"Sorry," he said. "Can't make it after all. Things are too busy over here."

I said nothing, but my silence spoke volumes.

"Come on, Kathy, you know how it is," Jerry said, an edge to his voice. "My company is always going to come before yours."

Something inside me snapped.

I will never depend on you again, I thought. From now on, I will stand on my own two feet.

I canceled the appointment with Jerry's banker, found a different bank and set up my own Line of Credit. The process was easy, as it turned out. In fact, when I really thought about it, from the moment

I first said yes to Qualis, yes to Jane, and even yes to China, I'd felt carried, protected, and in perfect alignment.

I'd jumped off a cliff, and instead of tumbling to certain death, the ground rose up to support me.

A few months later my mother came to stay for a few days. She shook me awake in the middle of the night. "The phone in my room won't stop ringing!" she complained. I discovered she had hung her pants over the FAX machine, and all the overnight China orders couldn't get through. Such was my glamorous existence as an international tycoon.

But my accounts kept growing and as orders kept pouring in, so did money. When my accountant laid out the company profits for our first fiscal year, I was astounded at the number of zeros. I couldn't wait to tell Jerry.

His reaction was not what I expected, not at first. He literally grew pale at the extent of my achievement. I hadn't asked for his help for some time, but he only now seemed to register this fact. I no longer depended on him.

He tried to regroup, applauding me with a few half-hearted claps. "Well, you go, girl," he said, but his face told a different story.

He never, ever expected me to be this successful, I realized. It's threatening to him! Anger flared. For all his encouragement, he was still caught in an old male-female paradigm. He needed me to need him, and this dynamic was not about to change, not as long as he and I were together. He would never accept me as an equal. The power exchange would always be skewed in his favor.

I said goodbye. I let Jerry go.

That night, I climbed into bed and glanced across at the soul painting.

"Happy now?" I asked, hugging a pillow to my aching chest.

Was it my imagination, or was the figure in the center ever so slightly more defined?

Every moment in time and space is you being reflected back to yourself from the particular point of view you choose to express at that particular moment.

—Bashar

Dear reader, as hard as it has been for me to accept sometimes, *everyone is a gift!*

Without the five guys, I might still be running in place, trapped in a hamster wheel of old ideas. They were grist for my mill. Their tendency to demean and diminish forced me to grow and change.

And Jerry, too, was a powerful source of learning for me. I'm not going to lie. Severing the bond with him was one of the hardest things I have ever done. Like many women, I mistook co-dependence for love, and saying goodbye to Jerry—to "us"—was truly painful. But as with the Five Guys, I've never lost sight of how grateful I am for those years with Jerry. I am deeply thankful for him—all of him, supportive and otherwise.

Because the truth is, every single one of us is simply a reflection of the other. We're all constantly beaming information back and forth, absorbing lessons and offering them back. It's no accident who or what comes into our sphere of influence. We land in each other's life for a reason.

What gifts has Spirit sent to you?

12

FINDING MY TRIBE

There is almost a sensual longing for connection with others who have a large vision. The immense fulfillment of the friendship between those engaged in furthering the evolution of consciousness has a quality impossible to describe."

—PIERRE TEILHARD DE CHARDIN

I had a new mission—to find like-minded souls, successful entrepreneurs who were committed to spiritual development and motivated by love.

I knew what I needed. I just didn't know if they existed, not until one sunny summer morning, a rare Saturday free from the nonstop work of running Qualis. I'd just celebrated year one of operations, and business was exploding. I sat on the patio leafing through a newsletter from the Institute of Noetic Sciences. IONS was a non-profit institution I'd recently discovered that promoted two areas close to my heart—science, and spirit.

A slight breeze riffled my hair. The summer sunshine gilded the smooth surface of the lagoon. My hand paused. Before my eyes could even convey the information to my brain, my heart knew. My life was about to change.

The magazine interview was with Willis Harman—Stanford Professor of Electrical Engineering, futurist, and visionary. A senior social scientist at the Stanford Research Institute, Harman had served as President of IONS since 1975. Normally his work addressed global transformation from the perspective of human consciousness, but this interview was different. This interview focused on business.

More specifically, something called the World Business Academy.

Apparently, a few years earlier Harman noticed that more and more businessmen were hanging out at the Research Institute, soaking up information. Their curiosity was motivated by the same question— could the principles of scientific and spiritual transformation apply to the practicalities of running a company?

My heart quickened as my eyes flew across the page.

Like a lot of people, Harman had long harbored a prejudice against "big business." He thought that corporations were a central cause of the world's problems, not a path to solutions. But he set aside his initial resistance and kept listening. After a time, Harman presented these forward-thinking businessmen with a challenge—if they were so interested in connecting commerce with spirituality for the purpose of uplifting humanity, why not found their own institute with that goal in mind?

In 1987—one year before Qualis came to be—the World Business Academy (WBA) was born, a nonprofit think tank focused on the role of business in personal and global transformation. Willis Harman was co-founder, along with corporate executive and entrepreneur Rinaldo Brutoco. Harman had come to realize how the innate power of business could be used as a force of good. Money was not intrinsically bad—on the contrary, channeled correctly, it could be transformative.

I gobbled the article in one bite before returning to the top to relish again each and every line. WBA was a network of executives and entrepreneurs with the mission of expanding global consciousness using business as a tool. They also shared a personal quest to discover deeper meaning in their lives.

Yes! I had experienced these very things myself! Qualis was already proving to be a vehicle for personal growth, as well as an opportunity to practice spiritual principles on a corporate scale.

Harman underlined the distinction between change—which happens constantly—and transformation, which is lasting. He brushed aside as too cynical the current trend of future-thinking as a method of predicting catastrophe. But he was no fan of the "woo-woo" perspective either—overly idealistic points of view purposely blind to scientific evidence. The Academy's approach did not discard the rational. It applied observable, alternative solutions to real-world problems, and encouraged the application of fundamental spiritual tools to promote transformation. In short, the WBA believed in the possibility of a radical paradigm shift in the way the world did business.

I looked up from the page, eyes shining. As both avid seeker and ambitious businesswoman, I had marched through the previous decade on a lonely road. Yes, I attended endless EST courses and human potential seminars and workshops and sessions with spiritual beings, but I was usually alone, and always consciously keeping such activities apart from my working world. I would rush to events straight from the office, still dressed in a business suit and high heels. When I looked around, I saw nothing but robes, beads and Birkenstocks. I would scour the rooms and think, "Where are the Capricorns? Where are the business people?"

I needed those spiritual mentors, don't get me wrong. Whether it was Shirley MacLaine or Bashar, each encounter was impactful, reinforcing my deepest values and strengthening core convictions. They set me on a soulful path and planted signposts of wisdom to guide the way forward.

I took note of powerful spiritual axioms like: "Every situation in life is neutral until you charge it with emotion, be it positive or negative." Or, "What you put out is what you get back." Or, "Every challenge is a gift, placed in your world for a reason."

I applied these universal principles to my role at Qualis as best I could. I kept an eye on emotional charges, positive or negative. I tried to adopt an attitude of listening and caring, of being of service and dealing fairly, of never taking advantage of my reps, and never lying or cheating or shortchanging buyers. I even did my best to feel grateful for the roadblocks. I so wanted my company to not only achieve quality and excellence in all things, but also be a spiritual force for good. But sometimes I felt as if I was making my way without a compass, a solo explorer in the world of conscious commerce.

On this bright and sun-dappled Saturday morning, something shifted, and the world warmed up. I had found my tribe. I was not alone.

I jumped up, ready and eager to dive right in. But it was Saturday. There was nobody to call.

By Sunday morning I couldn't wait a second longer. I called IONS and left a breathless message on their general voicemail. "This is Kathy Gardarian. Willis Harman *has* to call me. I *have* to know more about the World Business Academy!"

I hung up the phone and walked outside. Their headquarters were located in Burlingame, close to San Francisco. Almost close enough to touch.

Nice guy that he was, Willis called back first thing Monday morning. The longer we talked, the more he understood my excitement over WBA.

"I think you might be perfect for the academy," he said. "Let me put you in touch with Rinaldo Brutoco, WBA's president."

Rinaldo called soon after. I peppered him with questions, and he further described the goals and procedures of the academy. WBA board members gathered once a month, sometimes in Burlingame, sometimes in far-flung places for longer retreats, but always to tackle subjects concerning transformation and business, and to help each other grow in wisdom and knowledge.

"It sounds wonderful," I replied. "How do I join?"

He seemed to hesitate. "Well… There are certain requirements in order to qualify for membership."

"Okay…"

"First of all, you have to be the CEO of a company."

"I am," I answered. "I opened my own business, Qualis International, a year ago."

"Ah," he said. "The thing is, the company must do a minimum of two million a year in business."

"Already there," I said, and a seed of satisfaction bloomed in my chest. In fact, I was up to five million.

"You'll be our first woman," he warned.

"Nothing new about that! I'll feel right at home."

He invited me up to Burlingame for a face-to-face meeting.

I counted the days, fretting over what to wear as if I were going on a first date. I decided on a deep purple dress, the color of wisdom and ambition—the color a queen might choose.

Rinaldo was a bright charmer with a twinkle in his eyes and fire in his heart. We hit it off immediately. He later confessed that the moment he spotted me click-clicking across the room, purple dress swirling, he knew my involvement was meant to be.

I was the first woman member of the World Business Academy, and the first to join the board. In my twenty-two years as a board member, I never missed a meeting, flying from wherever I was to wherever they were. Often I shuttled up to Burlingame for the night. The longer board retreats would second as vacations, as we gathered in exotic locales. Finally, I had both motive and opportunity to travel all over the world!

Wherever we came together, we would spend hours exchanging fascinating leadership tales of self-improvement and human potential—our version of "shoptalk." We challenged ourselves with queries—How could we grow in consciousness? How could we meet adversity with love? We discussed the role of spirit in business, and the importance of ethical behavior, of transparency in all things.

I was in heaven! Here was a diverse group of like-minded individuals, business people in business suits from different walks of life and different arenas, all with the same bottom line as me. We measured success not just in dollars but spiritual growth. "Rich" meant inwardly full as well as outwardly prosperous. Each of us was committed to doing the inner work, and all of us believed that positive organizational change started with personal transformation.

The impact on my life was instant, and profound. The World Business Academy's mission was not only to foster wisdom, but also to disseminate what we'd learned. We all agreed—any change in culture had to start at the top. As founding trustees we used our monthly gatherings as think tanks—or better yet, *feel* tanks—to bring up specific challenges we were facing in the workplace. This was a vulnerable and in some cases unique experience for many of us—I recall one extremely high-powered CEO weeping the first time he opened up about a professional crisis.

At one such early meeting, Rinaldo included some outside guests—potential members. He moved locations to a building in downtown San Francisco, where the conference room had a large, oval table that could accommodate the group of twenty.

I scanned the rows of nametags, looking for mine, when another name—Landon Carter—stopped me in my tracks. Landon had been my original EST trainer, almost fifteen years earlier. Our trainers were like gods back then, and Landon had radiated that healthy, spiritual glow that epitomized enlightenment. Now his path, too, had led him here. Talk about past and present interconnecting.

Rinaldo sat at the far end of the table, three small Tibetan bowls set in front of him. I took a seat midway. The chairs around me filled up—a few more women today, which was nice. Then Landon sat down at the far end of the table. I went over to him.

"Landon! How are you?"

He recounted how after his EST days he had gone through a really difficult patch, traveling to India to find a guru, leaving his former life behind.

My goodness, I thought, as I returned to my seat. It's never over, this spiritual path we're all on. We never know what's around the corner.

Rinaldo lifted a small mallet.

Dong. Dong. Dong.

The room grew quiet.

"We're going to try something a little different today," he said. "I'd like us all to sit and meditate for a few minutes on the following question—Why is spirit in business important to you?"

Dong. Dong. Dong.

I decided I would focus on love, how everyone is a spark of the divine and it's important in business to practice loving-kindness.

Dong. Dong. Dong.

The speakers moved clockwise. All the answers were fascinating— so many different levels of understanding in one room!

Soon a man sitting directly across from Landon was in the hot seat.

"My name is Mike Blondell," he began. He was tall and broad-shoul- dered, a strong bear of a guy with a reddish blond beard and cropped hair. I couldn't see his face. My turn was almost up, and at first I listened with only half an ear.

But not for long.

"When I was a teenager," Mike said, "my life was really good. What- ever I wanted, I got. I never questioned anything." He paused. "Then I became a Navy SEAL. For those of you who don't know what that means, I was trained to kill people. And that's what I did."

Talk about getting my attention!

I wondered, How the hell do you start life killing people and end up at the World Business Academy?

"After I left the service, I joined the business world," he went on, as if reading my mind. "But pretty soon I realized something. We're doing the same thing in business as I did on the battlefield. We treat each other like enemies. We're still killers, trained to crush our competitors." Mike's voice broke. "It needs to stop. We need to transform the way we do business."

Whenever a man cries, it makes me cry. And for an ex-soldier to be that vulnerable? He must be digging very deep. Tears rolled down my cheeks.

I hurried up to him at the break. He was easy to spot—he towered over everyone else.

"That's quite a shift—from hand-to-hand combat Navy SEAL to being a business man," I said. "I mean, I can't imagine. What was that transition like?"

Mike's smile was pained. "Well, it's not as if I didn't do a lot of work in between the two," he said. "A lot of work, and a lot of therapy."

I took that in, touched to my core.

He opened up further. "The last one, the very last man I killed, something happened. I was in Viet Nam. We were both so young, that soldier and I. And there was this brief moment in time—barely a nanosecond—when we both knew. He knew he was going to die, and I knew I was going to live. And it was… it was as if we both knew we were just playing a part."

I said nothing.

"That flash of knowing?" he went on. "That's when I realized that this game of life was bigger than me, or him, or what any of us thought. We're all here playing these parts so that we can learn what we need to learn next."

What a perspective on life, and death.

Mike and I became dear friends. He truly had one of the sweetest hearts I've ever known. Years later, when he died in a tragic boating accident, his unique perspective brought solace to my grief. I realized it was his time, the accident his final part to play. Soon after, his wife gave me a painting she'd felt compelled to paint right after his death.

"I know Mike wants you to have this," she said.

She'd painted a portrait of a strong woman's face. Rays of white Christ-light surrounded her, radiating outward. Looking at it, I remembered Rosie's message from Spirit, how I chose to come to this life on the ray of love. It was as if Mike wanted to remind me of this—to stay on my path.

Not every WBA encounter was so serious.

One early WBA adventure took place in Hawaii, where we participated in a Shamanic fire ceremony held within a large tent on the Big Island. The day was steamy and we were told to dress accordingly, which is how I found myself in the midst of a sacred circle in a bathing suit. I'd only just become a board member—welcome to your new world, Kathy! Self-conscious, I shifted from foot to foot as a Talking Stick moved ever closer.

At last someone placed the stick in my hand. I grasped it, hoping for at least a tiny sliver of insight to share with my fellow academy members. Instead, I swayed in place, overwhelmed by a vision—a sense of knowing so deep it made me dizzy. I realized we had all been together as a group before, sharing truth with one another. But I also got a clear sense that we had been much more advanced way back when.

The power of love never changes, I thought, but human nature is forgetful. We learn the same wisdom-lessons over and over, grasping them close, only to carelessly let them go.

And here we were in Hawaii, starting over once again.

Everyone was waiting. "We've all been together before," I said, keeping the impatience out of my voice, and quickly thrust the Talking Stick to the next person.

Why couldn't the world retain this powerful message of love? What was wrong with us? We had so much to offer, and yet we remained stuck in this new humanity that wasn't nearly as evolved as we used to be!

Some months later, the academy held another long retreat at a beautiful country estate in Ascot, England. Rinaldo had set aside a block of time for the founding trustees to rework our mission statement, a task we'd been laboring over for months.

We'd already spent an entire hour arguing over the inclusion of the word "spirit."

"We don't want people to get the wrong idea," one member said.

"It's too… you know… mystical sounding," another added. "Why can't we stick with 'ethics in business?' We want to attract CEO's, remember? We don't want to turn them off."

"How about 'consciousness' instead of 'spirit'?" another jumped in. "That's more empowering, right?"

"I say, leave 'spirit' in."

"No, no, take it out."

"In…"

"Out…"

My frustration reached a boiling point. "How about we leave it in and trust that whoever is called to be here will show up?" I said. "If the word 'spirit' is too much for others, so what? They'll come later!" I got up and left the room. I needed a break.

Willis Harman was sitting outside in a lawn chair, quietly enjoying the fragrant night air. I'm sure I looked distraught. We Italians tend to wear our feelings on our faces. Willis cocked his head.

"What's wrong?" he asked.

I explained why I was feeling so annoyed, recounting for him my earlier vision in Hawaii. If anything, my conviction had only gotten stronger. "It's just…we all think we're so evolved, so smart!" I exclaimed. "But the truth is, we're not nearly as wise as we used to be."

"Patience, Kathy." Harman's voice was kind. "You must learn patience. You have the kind of mind that already sees where all this will lead to, where we are headed. And you're right. We're not there yet. We're not in the new paradigm." He shrugged, smiling. "But we're also not in the old. We're on a bridge, somewhere between the two. You want to run straight to the other side of the bridge. Wouldn't it be more loving to stand in the middle and help everyone else across?"

I thought about it for a hot second. "Nope," I said. "I intend to run to the other side, turn around and yell back to everyone how great it is!"

He laughed as he shook his head. "Patience," he said again. "You'll learn."

A list of desirable traits started to take shape. *Perspective* from Mike Blondell, *patience* from Willis Harman. And before very long, three more ingredients landed on my growing recipe for spiritual success.

This WBA trip took us to Mumbai, India. One sultry afternoon, a few of us paid a visit to Mahatma Gandhi's Bombay headquarters and home. The modest structure was a welcome pocket of calm in the midst of the feverish, honking bustle of Mumbai. I walked through the front gate leading to the house and was suffused with a profound sense of awe. What tales could these walls whisper?

I stepped inside. The ground floor was a small alcove featuring a bronze bust of Gandhi, draped with a simple silk shawl. I offered quiet thanks, and started up the stairs.

The staircase walls were sprinkled with snapshots of Gandhi's life, a trail of historic moments that led to more treasure—a first floor gallery replete with photographs, paintings, press clippings, and all matter of memorabilia. A series of glass-enclosed miniature set pieces marked key moments in his journey from birth to death.

I paused to marvel at a framed personal correspondence from another giant of the time. The letter was in German, but the signature was unmistakable in any language—A. Einstein. Gandhi and Einstein—two lions in their time.

But the top floor of the house—part gallery representing all the ashrams where Gandhi spent time, part private quarters—especially moved me. You could feel the power in the silence. Here was where Gandhi dreamed—where he meditated and planned and prayed and slept. The tiled floor and whitewashed walls breathed simplicity. Two handcrafted spinning wheels occupied one corner, and wooden prayer beads lay coiled on a floor-bed, humble as a monk's pallet. A pair of worn leather sandals rested at the foot of the bed, as if waiting. All that was lacking was Gandhi's own gaunt frame, but his spirit was there, permeating that sacred space.

As I descended the stairs, I glanced to my left. Someone—Gandhi?—had tacked a yellowing index card to a bulletin board affixed to the wall. It was like a recipe card, only this was a recipe for living, not cooking. Gandhi had handwritten this reminder, a spiritual prescription for success: Be truthful. Be gentle. Be fearless.

I rummaged in my purse for a pen and notebook—I collect quotations the way other people collect stamps. I copied the words as I pondered the phrases, one by one: *Be truthful. Be gentle. Be fearless.*

So simple. So searing.

Also, timeless—decades later, I would pass this wisdom along to a room full of businesswomen, as I accepted a lifetime achievement award from the National Association of Women Business Owners, along with the admission that then, as now, the biggest challenge for me remains to be fearless!

The Academy not only provided inspiration, it opened doors to new challenges. One day, a fellow member—the president of a boutique bank—reached out to me. He was the board president of the Institute for Transpersonal Psychology in Palo Alto.

"Kathy, I'm dying up here with all these scientists," he said. "They're great at research, but they're not business people. They don't understand fund-raising and they don't understand how to make good financial decisions. Join the board, please?"

Because I loved my friend, I said I'd do it. Soon after, at our urging, the Institute introduced a class on the role of spirituality in business. The woman organizing the course urged me to lead a session. "I can't find any women CEO's to participate," she said. "I figured this would be right up your alley."

I gave a short presentation on my experiences with Qualis, and my commitment to spirituality as a business tool. During the question and answer period, a young man's hand shot up.

"Yeah, so I've read your business résumé," he said. "Obviously you're very successful. What I want to know is, how do you reconcile your two gods?" His voice was laced with skepticism. "How can you possibly serve both the god of business and the god of love?"

I was startled by the prejudice, if not ignorance implied by his question. This was the Institute for Transpersonal Psychology, for goodness sake! But then I recalled how even Willis Harman had harbored suspicions about big business before founding WBA.

Like any good salesperson, I answered the young man's question with a question of my own. "Sounds as if you are having trouble accepting the concept of abundance?" I began. "Here's the thing. Business is one of the most powerful institutions on the planet today. Unlike other bureaucracies and organizations, businesses can make quick decisions—turn on a dime when they need to. And once a business connects its abundance with the desire to do good, the benefit to others grows exponentially." I opened my arms wide. "Business is not unspiritual! And by the way, this is an abundant universe. It's already all here—you just have to manifest your role in the world. It's not about lack. It's not about less. And it's certainly not about *not* loving God, or *not* living with love!"

His expression was still doubtful, but several others in the class nodded and smiled. Still, I had to mentally shake my head. Even here—at an institute devoted to personal transformation—old, tired ideas about spirit and success continued to exist.

As for me, I sought out wisdom wherever I could find it. My one-woman business was exploding, and I needed all the help I could get. Some months after I joined WBA, I had the rare opportunity to consult with an especially wise mind, at just the right time.

It was early October, 1989. Rinaldo called, very excited.

"The Dalai Lama is in Newport Beach this week," he said.

"I know, isn't it great?" It was all over the local news, and I was already planning on going to his talk.

"Then you probably also know the East-West Foundation sponsored his trip over here. Well, I just found out they are having a private dinner for only forty people at the Heinz residence."

(Yes, that Heinz—ketchup-scion Heinz.)

"That's practically in my back yard."

"That's why I called. The foundation reserved a few spots for our members. Are you interested? Dinner includes an opportunity to meet with His Holiness."

"You mean, one-on-one?"

"That's right."

"I'm in."

The synchronicity was not lost on me. I was on the horns of a very particular work dilemma at the time.

Only days before this conversation, the Dalai Lama had won the Nobel Peace prize for his tireless work on behalf of Tibet, and in opposition to the oppressive Chinese regime. Earlier in the summer, China's lethal imposition of martial law had led to the deaths of over three thousand of the country's best and brightest students, mowed down as they staged a protest in Tiananmen Square. Like so many, I was heartbroken by the massacre, and furious over the Chinese government's subsequent denial of the events.

Meanwhile, the international import branch of my business was booming. Every month Qualis shipments arrived in the United States from Hong Kong, the containers filled with products hand-made by Chinese workers in Chinese factories.

My friends had all weighed in. "Kathy!" they cried. "How can you keep doing business with China? You have to stop! You need to take a stand for human rights!"

I didn't disagree. I was horrified by the unfolding events. I wept at the photograph of a lone man standing, arms raised, as a massive tank bore down on him. He embodied the courage of the human spirit in the face of oppression. "No more!" he seemed to say, and my heart echoed that cry for freedom.

I wanted to take a moral stand and end my dealings with China. But frankly, I didn't know how. The logistics were a nightmare. Home Depot was opening 246 stores a year, and I was not only servicing these new stores, I also had to keep all the old ones supplied. Half my product orders were fulfilled in China, and on any given week I had dozens of containers making their way across the ocean, a journey that took at least thirty days to complete each way. The ships were in constant motion.

I'd been pondering this problem for months now—how to stop doing business in China without running out of product and letting down my primary client. Massive backorders would be a disaster for Home Depot, and therefore Qualis. Was terminating the relationship even the right decision?

Who better to ask than the Dalai Lama?

The Heinz residence was beautiful—Mediterranean on the outside, Art Deco once you stepped inside. We enjoyed a buffet dinner, rubbing shoulders with Southern California's industrial leaders. The Dalai Lama sat cross-legged on a sofa, a bright spot of saffron in the room, and answered questions as we ate.

"How can we introduce more spirituality into business?" one man asked.

"Work within the context of your own culture," he answered. He gestured at his saffron and burgundy robes. "No need for robes!" When the laughter died down, he continued. "It is always kindness and compassion that leads to human solutions."

Dinner passed pleasantly enough, but my eyes were trained on the diminutive monk as he moved through the room, spending a few minutes with each guest.

Finally it was my turn. He took the seat by my side.

When I asked how he was, he chuckled. "I can't keep my eyes open," he said. "I've been up since four in the morning, that's my meditation time. 7:30 feels like midnight to me."

I hadn't expected him to be so accessible and genuine, not to mention funny.

I got to the point. "Your holiness, I have a question for you, something that's been troubling me." I explained my dilemma, going into great detail—the new import business, the containers, the massacre at Tiananmen Square. He listened with friendly attention.

"What do I do? Should I cancel my orders?" I asked.

The Dalai Lama stood and took both my hands in his. "Kathy, why would you punish the Chinese people further, for the thoughts and actions of a few?"

My face must have reflected my surprise.

"China will be free one day," he explained. "It might take five years, it might take ten—the length of time doesn't matter. What does matter is that freedom is an idea whose time has come."

I nodded, still uncertain. "So, I shouldn't take a stand against the government's oppression?"

His eyes bored into mine. "You should never think about what you *don't* want. All you have to do is put your attention into the pool of consciousness that you *do* want to see. Act like it's already happened. That's how you create your own reality."

The room wavered and then sharply came into focus. The Dalai

Lama leaned back and smiled, as if he could tell—his words had moved me into a completely new understanding of what to do, and how to be.

"Wow," I said. "What a simple shift. I get it. If I pull my business out of China, I am giving power to the very people I don't want to empower. They've already harmed the students. Now they'd be hurting the factory workers as well."

Qualis was doing about three million U. S. dollars of business with that one factory per year. We were their biggest client. Losing our contract would be devastating, putting hundreds of workers, mostly women, out of work.

"Don't punish the people," the Dalai Lama repeated. "Keep acting as if they are going to be free, and keep empowering the people you need to empower."

"Thank you," I said. "I am traveling to Beijing next month. I shall remember your words."

He cocked his head, and his eyes twinkled. "One more thing. Remember to watch your tonality when you're there," he said.

"My tonality?"

"Yes. The Chinese are very sensitive to tone."

A month later, I stepped off the plane to face a row of guards wielding bayonets.

The uniformed customs official barraged me with questions, his voice harsh. "Who are you? Show me your passport! Why are you here?"

I kept a short leash on my temper.

The trip to Beijing was a gift from my manufacturer, a private sightseeing tour of the city arranged for me and a few other clients. Everywhere we went, we were required to show our passports, including, of course, Tiananmen Square. Our assigned guide was a lovely young Chinese woman, but she wouldn't—couldn't—discuss the massacre, because it "never happened."

"I'm being watched all the time," she told me at one point, her voice low.

Oppression has its own perfume. The scent of death was every-where in that city. People scurried past our group without raising their eyes. Windows and souls were both shuttered, as if to fend off outside dangers. America felt very far away.

I kept imagining the parents, what it must have felt like to them, the day their children didn't come home.

One afternoon I glimpsed what appeared to be a fabric store on the second floor of a ramshackle structure. Fabric is like catnip for me—irresistible. I darted across the street and pushed open the front door. The tiny alcove inside was dark, but not so dark that I couldn't make out a bristling circle of bayonets.

The ring of soldiers scowled, weapons pointed. One of them ges-tured with the blade end of his bayonet, eyebrows raised in question.

"Come on, guys! This is a fabric store!" I said, waving my arms wide.

So much for watching my tonality.

I ran up the stairs, the nape of my neck prickling at the thought of those razor-sharp tips. As I wove through aisles of shelving piled with embroidered silks, I didn't register a single thread. My heart was pounding too hard.

I waited for at least a half hour. When I finally left, the soldiers were gone.

Once our Chinese manufacturing operation was running smoothly, Home Depot gave me another thinly veiled ultimatum. They'd been pressing me for some time to become a distributor as well as a manu-facturer's rep, but so far I had successfully resisted shipping products directly to their individual stores. I much preferred relying on their built-in distribution centers and shipping networks.

Every few months, Jane would call.

"You have to store-door deliver."

"I can't."

"You have to."

"Nope. Sorry."

All I could think about was all those Home Depot stores—hundreds and hundreds of them carpeting the entire United States. Delivering product to each store directly was a daunting proposition, and I knew it would utterly change my life.

"Look, Kathy," Jane finally said, "if you don't start shipping directly to our stores, we'll find someone who will."

I needed a business partner, and fast, someone to manage the distribution arm of Qualis—locate appropriate warehouses, oversee truckers, keep track of delivery schedules, and a host of other as-yet-unknown tasks. Luckily I knew just the person—a young man of impeccable ethics and boundless energy—easy-going, patient, and wise beyond his twenty-four years. This trustworthy, talented soul also happened to know me better than anyone else on this planet.

He, too, was a member of my tribe—in this case a longstanding little tribe of two.

I invited my son Leo to join me at Qualis.

Love is the force that ignites the spirit
And binds teams together.

—Phil Jackson

Dear reader, I hope that you, too, have had the good fortune to *seek like-minded souls.* For me, this didn't mean people who always agreed with me, but rather people who shared my intentions and lovingly kept me honest! Where would I be without my tribe? These loving friends and spiritual lions became colleagues in battle and collaborators in consciousness. They helped me work through hard decisions, and nurtured my strengths. To this day I collect their wisdom like nuggets of gold, and their insights serve as portholes to future possibilities, and as fair-minded mirrors, reflecting the current reality.

If spirituality is not your primary focus, not to worry! There are plenty of mentors living with integrity and practicing authenticity who have chosen a more traditional path. As long as they lead with love, you are in good hands

Do I experience the occasional bout with fear or impatience? Of course I do! I still see things, sense things, and my first impulse is to stomp my feet and yell answers from wherever I stand. I still wonder why transformation takes so long? Why don't people recognize the truth? But then I look back at my own bumpy path and realize every journey takes whatever time it takes.

It's an inside job. Always was, always will be.

That's why we need to find our tribes and stay open to the teachers that come into our lives (whether we always like their lessons or not). I bow to them all, these bright souls whose lives have had such a lasting impact on me.

How about you? Who are the members of your tribe? How do they keep you honest?

13

MIRROR, MIRROR

**How do you call yourself, when
you want your soul to answer?**

—DAWNA MARKOVA

Spirit's curriculum can show up in odd and surprising ways. The greatest lesson of all, for me, ended as it began long ago.

With toilet paper.

Let me back up. Early on at Westcom, my boss Jerry had walked me through all the available paper goods items I could have in my portfolio.

"Here's a perfect product for you," he said at one point. "Toilet paper."

My answer was immediate. "No thank you. Toilet paper is boring."

"It may be boring, but everyone uses it," Jerry retorted.

"I don't care. I don't want toilet paper on my résumé." I shuddered inside. I might have left my dental receptionist job far behind, but my squeamishness had never left me.

"I'll pass, thanks," I said.

I assumed that was that, but I hadn't accounted for Spirit's dark sense of humor.

The World Business Academy's mission was not only to foster wisdom, but also to disseminate what we'd learned. We all agreed—there could be no organizational shift without personal transformation. Moreover, any change in culture had to start at the top. As founding trustees we used our monthly gatherings as think tanks—or better yet, *feel* tanks—to bring up specific challenges we were facing in the workplace. This was a vulnerable and in some cases unique experience for many of us—I recall one CEO with tears in his eyes the first time he opened up about a professional crisis with which he was grappling.

We tried to make our lofty goals specific: How could we actually become better, wiser CEOs? What particular decisions might help us lead with love? When should we say yes, and when, no, in order to strengthen our ethics, and instill our choices with spirit? Part training program, part feedback loop, we used these meetings of likeminded colleagues to hold our ethical feet to the fire.

As for me, give me a room full of likeminded CEOs and I could talk for hours about the transformational power of love in the workplace. Actually *practicing* openhearted acceptance every day? That proved to be a different story, especially with regards to one particular colleague of mine. This ongoing interpersonal nightmare forced me to put my spiritual money where my mouth was and ultimately to learn that only if I "walked the talk," could radical shifts happen.

Which brings me to the story of David.

I knew of David—you might say his reputation preceded him—although he and I didn't professionally cross paths during the first seven years of Qualis. He was a top buyer for the merchandising side of Home Depot, while I was a vendor for their expense division. "Resale" merchandisers stocked the shelves with home improvement products, while the expense division bought in-store goods that serviced customer needs. The merchandisers got big bonuses for their fancy catalogue items. Not so, the expense vendors. Naturally, Home Depot's main focus was on goods and products, and management treated the expense division like an inconvenient stepchild. The two cultures were completely different, and the Atlanta headquarters even housed the divisions in two separate buildings, connected by a pedestrian bridge.

David embodied the macho, arrogant ideal of the resale division. He was a gruff, Type-A personality who used his thick New York accent like a bludgeon. He intimidated and bullied others to get what he wanted.

Not exactly my ideal of enlightened business behavior.

My woman buyer at Home Depot could be difficult at times, but Jane and I had a very amicable working relationship. We'd been together for years, and more than once I'd told her how grateful I was to report to her, and not David.

Then she left the company.

I got the heads-up from a fellow rep at the Depot.

"Bad news," she said. "David's your new purchaser."

My heart sank. I recalled another acquaintance at the Depot. Her nickname was the Apron Lady, since she was in charge of the account that provided the sales force's ubiquitous orange Home Depot aprons. We became friends. One time she had even called me in tears, after an especially challenging meeting with David.

I thought about the way he hunched his body, as if he was a victim, not a perpetrator. How his gruff manner affected others.

I called my son Leo. "I think we may have to let Home Depot go."

"What are you talking about? They're our biggest account."

"I don't know if I can work with my new buyer," I said. "Leo, I've met this guy a bunch of times and he still acts like I'm a complete stranger. He can't even look me in the eye!"

"Mom…" Leo was using his "reasonable" voice, the one he adopts when he thinks I'm overreacting.

But I was on a roll. "Maybe it's because I'm a woman. Maybe he has a difficult relationship with his mother or something, but he behaves like a misogynist. He'll make my life miserable."

"At least meet with him," Leo said. "You never know."

I agreed, reluctantly, but I did know. My mind was already set. I was in for a complicated future if I stuck with David. I envisioned the absolute worst—and no, the Dalai Lama would not have approved.

David was still working out of the merchandising division. Our initial meeting brought me inside that hallowed building for the first time. The waiting room was huge, sunlit and gorgeous. Quite the contrast—over on the expense side we were ushered into tiny windowless cells to wait for appointments. I'd flown four thousand miles to get here, and I sunk into a plush seat. Jetlag battled with dread at what was to come. To distract myself, I perused the surroundings. My eyes were pulled to the opposite wall. A giant painted rendition of the Home Depot mascot, "Homer D. Poe," loomed. Homer is a cartoon character complete with bulbous nose, workman's cap, orange apron, and loaded tool belt, kind of a next-door neighbor, Do-It-Yourself guy. To this day he graces the brochures, buttons, and bags of many a Home Depot store.

This Homer wasn't wearing a tool belt. He was wearing a gun belt. Not only that, his holster was empty. Both guns were drawn. One raised muzzle dribbled a trail of smoke, evidence of a recent shot. The second barrel projected a balloon caption containing the threatening message "BEWARE! You are entering the merchandising side of Home Depot."

Great, I thought. There go my profit margins.

I'd heard that these resale guys were competitive, but no one told me they self-identified as gunslingers.

Moments later, David appeared in the doorway to collect me. He slouched to my side, his head lowered.

"Hello, David," I said, my voice bright with false hope.

"Hey, howya doin," he muttered to the floor. "Let's do this in the conference room." I followed him around the corner to a large glass-enclosed meeting space. He fumbled with a key. A small sign to the left of the door caught my eye. It didn't say 'Conference Room.' It said 'War Room.'

That did it. I started to laugh.

David froze, key in hand. "What's so funny?"

"Come on," I said, still smiling. "Homer with his guns blazing? War room? I'm just here to talk about bags and packaging."

He unlocked and entered without another word.

Once we'd settled inside, David explained that the Depot had shifted him to the expense department to "clean things up," and he needed to familiarize himself with everything having to do with Qualis.

He peppered me with questions. What was our national program? Where did we store our products? What did we specifically have to offer in the way of savings?

I tried to keep up, explaining the specific programs, itemizing our extensive product list.

David started to wriggle and squirm in his seat, as if he couldn't get comfortable.

He doesn't want to move to the expense division, I realized. He still wants to be a cowboy.

The meeting was unbearably long, and I soon picked up on a pattern—he'd half-listen to an explanation, decide he understood without fully grasping the material, and interrupt with a random question on a completely different subject. It's a chaotic way to do business, like trying to negotiate while sitting in a hailstorm.

A merchandising colleague strode past the conference room, glancing inside automatically. He stopped and backed up, agog, as if he'd spotted a rare species of parrot or something. But the uncommon bird was me—a woman! In the war room!

He yelled through the glass, "Hey, David! Are ya' closing a big deal in there?"

David visibly puffed his chest, like a Bantam rooster. "You got it!" he called out. "This is huge! I'm trying to decide if I should order one-ply or two-ply toilet paper in here!"

My body stiffened as I held back the anger. Toilet paper? Again? I'd thought I was done with it, but here I was, publicly, mockingly connected to a product I loathed. And by the way, why *did* Jerry assume toilet paper was my kind of product? Something told me it was gender-related.

The man outside smirked, and gave David a double thumbs-up.

Okay, maybe the plaque outside wasn't so off after all. David was my enemy. This was war.

David and I met at least once a month. I soon recognized his favorite tools for bargaining. We all have them—automatic behaviors, often unconscious—but his were easy for me to spot.

They came in threes, his ABCs for getting his way.

First, *Attack.* He'd lead with confrontation and get right in my face—yelling, badgering, and complaining about my work.

Second, *Bargain.* He'd calm down enough to actually negotiate, so we could hammer out a deal and complete our agenda.

Finally, *Compliment.* The moment we'd brokered an agreement, he'd drop any sign of aggression and move into flattery mode. "Don't worry about a thing," he'd say, patting my arm. "You're doing a really good job."

By then, I was too beaten up to care.

And every month I complained to the academy.

"You won't believe what he did this time," I would bitch, my claws fully extended. I'd let loose, rat-a-tat-tatting my CEO friends with horror stories, every meeting, a new insult. I vacillated between crushed and furious.

But one month, I noticed they weren't responding to my list of wrongs with the usual murmurs of support. I tried again.

"It's like he thrives on shock value! 'Me big buyer, you peon vendor,' right?"

Nothing.

"I just, I just..." I hesitated for a moment but then I plowed ahead. "I actually feel hatred for this man."

My words landed like lumps of bitter coal. I was shocked at how bitter I had become. "I think I have to leave the Depot," I said, realizing. "I can't deal with David any longer."

After a moment, somebody spoke—I don't remember who but it doesn't matter. He was a mouthpiece for the collective wisdom of the group.

"I have two questions for you, Kathy," he said. "First, do you think David is another aspect of the Divine? Take your time. Really think about this."

I closed my eyes. I pictured David's face, twisting with anger as he yelled at me. I opened my eyes and looked around at all my buddies.

"Nope," I said. "I might be one with all of you. But I am *not* one with him."

Laughter rippled around the room.

"God may be all powerful, but She made a mistake this time," I added.

Another board member piped up. "We know that you know better, Kathy," he said, as the others nodded. "On a deep level, you know better than that."

"Here's the second question," the first man said. "There are only two real emotions—love, and fear. Which do you think David is coming from?"

I knew what he was implying, but I didn't want to go there, not yet. I settled for, "He's certainly not very loving."

"So you're saying fear is the truth of him?"

This question stopped me. I truly believe that we are all born in love. Wordsworth put it perfectly, "trailing clouds of glory as we come, from God who is our home." Once alive, we are inundated with experiences. We pile all this stuff on top of that glory. It's not that the love in a person's heart has evaporated. You just can't see it. It's as if that purity has been smeared over with gunk, like a thick layer of peanut butter. It's too dense to penetrate. We can't come from love anymore, because the love can't seep through.

"No," I answered, my voice quiet. "Fear is not the truth of him."

My WBA friends laid out a new plan of action for me, one motivated by love instead of fear. "You leap into reaction-mode every time you're with David," they said. "Clearly, rather than getting you anywhere, it's making you miserable."

I couldn't argue with that.

"You need to let your higher self do business with his higher self."

I must have grimaced.

"Kathy, you know he has one," he added. "A part of him that's impeccable, so much more than the face he shows. Every time you walk into a room, and David is there, we want you to literally beam him love. You don't have to say a word. Just create the field of energy that you want for yourself."

I remembered Mahatma Gandhi—how he urged us to become the change we wanted to see in the world. Powerful words. And here was the identical message—different channel, same truth.

"He will never institute the change himself," they pointed out. "*You* have to change. Your choice. Your field."

On the flight home, my body grew as stiff and resistant as a block of wood.

I have to beam him love? Who do they think I am, Mother Teresa?

Still, I knew my fellow board members were right. I knew that the harder I pushed back, the harder things would be. What you resist persists, right? But I also knew from experience that the more difficult the challenge, the more transformational the result.

I had to at least try.

My first test run with David was almost immediate—isn't that always the way? You commit to a shift of behavior and boom! The exact situation shows up, right in your face.

Most of our product line with Home Depot was resin-based. The cost of manufacturing resin is notoriously volatile, changing all the time. I no sooner came home from the WBA meeting than the price of resin jumped almost five cents per pound, affecting virtually every item of our portfolio. I must have forwarded David twenty letters from manufacturers, each one noting a cost increase. Resin was in everything—merchandise bags, pallet wrap covers, trunk liners for the car, even the giant rolls of plastic used to protect carpeting, when customers transported their yards of floor covering home. I kept faxing David the higher prices, reminding him with every cover letter, "This isn't me speaking—the price increase is coming from our manufacturers."

I faxed David the bad news. And then I waited for the tantrum I knew was coming.

He called late in the day, apoplectic.

"Hello, David," I said, trying to remember to breathe. *Don't be reactive, Kathy. Don't be reactive.*

"WHAT IS THIS CRAP?"

"Well, did you get all the manufacturers' letters explaining about the resin increase?"

"I DON"T CARE! WE'RE THE DEPOT AND WE'RE NOT TAKING A PRICE INCREASE! I NEED YOU TO COME INTO THE OFFICE RIGHT AWAY!"

I was already tired from the trip up north—deep inner work can be exhausting. Worse, I had woken up that day with a cold. But I didn't push back, or dig in my heels. I booked an Atlanta flight for the next morning, determined to give this new approach a try.

The next afternoon I found myself sitting in the windowless cubicle that passed as a waiting room—no merchandiser's spacious lobby for me this time. A locked door separated me from the buyers' meetings taking place on the other side of the wall. I felt like I was back in elementary school, waiting outside the principal's office, in trouble again for playing hooky.

So far, my magic love-beaming mechanism had yet to fully kick in.

Stay open, I thought. Create a different field of energy.

The door opened, and I looked up, expecting David's dour face. But instead, I saw an unexpected but happy surprise—the Home Depot Apron Lady! We had become friends over time, and she was a sight for sore eyes. Talk about synchronicity—if ever I needed a buddy, someone to remind my heart of its capacity to love, it was now. Her eyes lit up when she saw me.

"Kathy!" she exclaimed. "How are you? How great to see you! What are you doing here?"

I told her about my emergency summons. "So, did you just have an appointment with David?" I asked.

"Yes…" she said, her voice a little guarded.

"Is he in a good mood?"

She glanced at the door as if it had ears. "Well… he can be difficult to do business with."

"Don't I know it," I said.

And then she said something astonishing. "But at least he likes *you*."

I had to laugh. "Really?" I said. "Tell me more, because that hasn't been my experience."

My friend was incredulous. "Are you kidding? It's totally true! David talks about you all the time. How you had the guts to start your own business. How you're one of the few female-owned companies that do business with the Depot. He has so much respect for you."

I looked at the Apron Lady as if she were an angel. Her words were like magic, and my icy resistance to David started to melt, like icicles in springtime

We hugged goodbye. "Thank you," I said. "You have no idea how much you just helped me."

I sat down again. Hopefully David wouldn't come get me until I had time to fully process this new information.

That little SOB, I thought. He's liked me this whole time, and still he puts me through all this?

But I was smiling, because I now had two trump cards. In one pocket, the knowledge that David not only liked me, he respected me—something he would never ever admit to, but still. And in the other, the academy's sage advice, to meet his higher self with my own.

Okay, I thought. Bring it on.

**Change the story and you change perception;
change perception and you change the world.**

—JEAN HOUSTON

Dear reader, I believe in synchronicity. I've had too many "strange coincidences" happen throughout my life not to. But synchronicity needs a fertile field in which to flourish. That's why I need to *practice willingness*, or in other words, to stay teachable.

How many times, when I shift my attitude from resistant to open, have unexpected solutions arrived? If I dig in my heels, nothing can change. Only when I am open to learning and growing does Spirit have room to do her work!

It's as if willingness is the prerequisite to transformation.

When the Apron Lady came through that door and delivered her message, I understood that I was back in the flow of spirit.

Have you noticed this in your life as well, dear reader? Can you recollect moments at work, as well as elsewhere, when willingness opened the door to unexpected synchronicity and support?

14

WALKING THE TALK

**"If you treat an individual as he is, he will remain
how he is. But if you treat him as if he were
what he ought to be and could be, he will
become what he ought to be and could be."**

—JOHANN WOLFGANG VON GOETHE

I sat down across from David. Same meeting room. Same pair of adversaries. But this time a loosened framework allowed just enough space for something different to happen.

I can't say it was easy. I stared at my nemesis and wondered, *Is he really an aspect of the divine?*

Yes, my heart replied. Maybe not the best representation, but yes. An aspect.

And don't forget, my head chimed in. He actually respects you.

Beam him love. Do business with his higher self. Focus on the divine.

David knew none of this, of course. He was barking about everything, as usual. No one would ever suspect that he held me in high esteem—far from it. But the relationship had shifted. The beans were spilled. I could no longer rest in my comfortable state of resentment.

I lasted about ten minutes that first time, before slipping into reaction over some ridiculously irritating thing he said. Expressing radical, unconditional love toward David was like learning to use a brand new muscle—it took constant practice, and I had to start small.

But every phone call, every meeting, even when the mere thought of him crossed my mind, I would beam the love, build the muscle.

Often I'd have to stop, mid-conversation. "Hang on a minute, David. I have another call." And I'd literally put him on hold.

This is a neutral situation, Kathy. How are you going to handle it? Are you going to make it worse, or better? Charge it with negative, or positive emotion? It's completely up to you.

Once I felt centered, I'd continue the call, stronger than before.

I began to realize something profound. Love is an active choice. I *made a decision*—I am going to love David for the way he is, and the way he is not. No conditions. No expectations. If he goes through his Attack-Bargain-Compliment waltz, so be it. I'm right there. If he drops the dance and decides to do business in a calm, straightforward manner, I'm right there, too.

Day after day, I practiced showering unconditional love on David. The more I practiced, the stronger the muscle, and the stronger the muscle, the easier it was to love him without limitation.

It was harder when we weren't in the same room. Face to face, I could sense his energy, read it almost like a weather report. But long distance, every time he would pause I could feel my stomach tighten—was he about to go in to a screaming match, or was he just taking a breath?

All I could do was wait, and try to stay centered.

One Friday afternoon—it was four o'clock my time, which meant seven o'clock in Atlanta—David called me. I wasn't sure if he was at work or at home, but either way I knew it was probably trouble. Late Friday calls were rare, and usually meant something needed fixing.

I was pretty sure I knew what was coming. On Monday I had an appointment with one of my Southern California bag manufacturers. David and I had met him a few times, and we both liked him a lot personally. Recently, however, he'd displayed the disconcerting habit of telling us he'd dispatched trucks with merchandise before they'd actually been manufactured. Home Depot was adding stores at an explosive rate, and we had to know the when and where of product distribution with absolute clarity. I really needed my manufacturers to perform, to do what they said they were going to do. Otherwise, we might run out of essential in-store items and have to backorder them.

This particular vendor would leave me cheery messages," No problem, Kathy! Trucks are on the way," and I would come to learn he hadn't even made the product yet. I'd left a message for David, giving him a heads-up. Much as we both liked him, either this vendor needed to shape up, or I would have to let him go.

I was sure David was calling to respond—I just had no idea how. Would he go ballistic on the vendor, guns blazing? Would he blame me for the problem? Would he undermine my authority and shrug things off because he liked the guy, a case of "What else can I do?"

Leo had come into my office to sit in on the call. I put David on speaker.

"Hi David. Just so you know, Leo's in the room."

David was silent at first. I lowered my shoulders and remembered to breathe.

"You know that appointment on Monday?" he finally said.

"Yes."

"I don't want you to blow the guy out of the water. I want you to see if we can fix this and make it work."

David's voice was calm. No screaming? What happened to *Attack?*

"I agree," I said, equally reasonable. "I plan on telling him, 'I don't want you to call me and tell me what I want to hear. I need to know about your actual production schedule, and is it working?' Either he'll commit to changing things, or we'll find another supplier."

More silence. What was coming next? I never knew. Then…

"Kathy, you know how sometimes you come in a room, and things seem to calm down?"

I stared at the phone.

"Do that," David said.

I looked at my son, and he looked at me, as if neither of us could believe our ears.

"He's *feeling* me changing," I told Leo, after the call ended and I'd double-checked with my son that yes, David had actually said those words. "He's feeling me loving him unconditionally, even if he doesn't know how to articulate it!"

And the shift in our relationship was lasting. Over time, David expanded our Home Depot portfolio to include more and more products, working with Leo and me to build up our business. He literally made Qualis the success it is today.

David still loved to tease me, calling me "the Bag Lady," but now his words came from a place of affection and respect.

He trusted me, trusted us. He would fax over proposals and let us source our own manufacturers. He believed in Qualis, and we didn't let him down. As we took on more products, David, too, was flourishing. The Depot made him responsible for all travel arrangements and telephone operations. Soon he had his own assistant. One day Leo and I met the two of them at a restaurant in Laguna Beach for lunch.

David nudged his assistant. "Can you believe these are our vendors?" he asked. "They're so great! They're authentic. They're real. They always do what they say they're going to do. I can always depend on them."

Wow, I thought. You can't buy compliments like this. Talk about powerful PR.

Qualis, my inner voice added. *This is why you started it.*

I wish I could say that David permanently became a saint, or that I did. Sadly, sometimes he would revert to old behaviors with other vendors in front of me. Sadly, I would judge him for it. But he never again treated me, or my company, with contempt.

I just had to see the good in him—the God in him. Recognize that I was dealing with another aspect of the divine. Drop all my judgments, and simply love him, the way he was, as well as the way he wasn't.

Everyone at the Depot was amazed. We became very close, so close that I went to both of his daughters' bat mitzvah's, and both of their weddings. "You're here!" he'd exclaim, greeting me at the door. "This wouldn't be the same without you. You're family."

"I'm giving you a new product to sell," David announced one afternoon in his office, a glint in his eye. "It'll be huge."

Something was up, I could tell.

"Really." I drew the word out, my eyebrows raised. "What kind of product?"

"Any kind I want," he retorted, but his eyes twinkled. We both had come to enjoy the banter.

"No, David. Not *any* kind you want. Because you know me—I like quick turnarounds, merchandise that moves. I don't want any big dogs taking up space in my warehouse."

"It's worth five million a year. Just saying…"

I let him sit, as if I wasn't interested, which we both knew was a total bluff. A product line worth five million? *Of course* I was interested!

"Okay," I relented. "What do you have in mind?"

David's turn to make me wait, as a grin spread slowly across his face.

"Toilet paper," he said.

The whole purpose of life is to bring love into existence where it is needed.

—BARRY LONG

Dear reader, if you take only one thing to heart from this book, let it be this—*lead with love.*

What a huge and humbling practice this was for me. What an awakening! I thought I was so enlightened, but spirituality had always been on my own terms. Even Deepak Chopra had me pegged. "Oh, I get it, Kathy," he teased. "You think this stuff only works if you *like* someone!" I got the same feedback from every direction.

My friend, we can't just spout these laws of the universe, we have to embody them! We need to be authentic and real, not just a mouthpiece for spiritual platitudes. And there is no more powerful tool for change than love, not only in life but also in our workplace.

It's a universal truth. People do business with people they like. Or to put it another way—business is relationships! When there is more space for the human spirit in the equation, the results are rewarding, productive, and profitable. Within each of us lies the power to transform relationships by leading with love. All we have to do is open our hearts.

My experience with David taught me how powerful loving

attention is, and how tangible its affect on others. We are all beams of energy, and when we walk into any space or situation, that energy precedes us.

David himself said it—"You know how sometimes you come in a room, and things just seem to calm down? Do that."

Do that—such simple words, to contain such a profound and life-altering message. And yet unconditional love worked, where nothing else did.

The irony is, all of this came from me wanting to retreat. I was convinced the only solution was to leave the situation. But I stood there, tall and proud as a woman. I refused to be impacted, and *that* David respected.

Imagine leaving such a huge lesson!

But this lesson was about so much more. Without the practice of love, without honoring David's soul and recognizing the divine in him, none of the profound changes that followed could have happened.

Have you tapped into the positive power of leading with love? When in your life has love transformed a difficult situation when nothing else could?

15

BEFRIENDING THE FEMININE

I was surrounded by wise men—academy members and friends like Rinaldo and Mike Blondell and another brilliant entrepreneur and enlightened businessman, Jim Cusumano. My son, Leo. But where, oh where, were the wise women? If I was to be a fountain of living water to nourish the feminine in others, hadn't I better know at least *one* flowing fountain myself?

As it was, I felt impatient with anybody who didn't take responsibility for their life, and that included quite a few women. Then Rosie and the soul painting happened, and I was forced to find a new way forward.

I soon found myself longing for a different kind of soul mate. A sister. Someone from whom I could learn, and with whom I could laugh and cry and build memories. A female friend I could love unconditionally. I still had some childhood scars around women and issues of trust. I was ready to remove them.

One summer evening a year or so after I started my company, I attended the Whole Life Expo at the Hilton Hotel next to LAX. I had a particular event in mind, a talk by an accomplished woman who had authored several books on psychosocial healing and human possibility. I hurried into the hotel ballroom a few minutes late (not every EST lesson took!). I slipped into the back row just as the speaker was introduced.

"...please welcome Jean Houston."

A tall, dark-haired figure stepped onto the stage. Like a bolt of electricity, the force of her presence arced across the crowded room and connected with my heart. She began to speak, and her words surged with power and authenticity. Plus, she had a raucous sense of humor. I sat entranced.

I must know this woman.

After the event I devoured her writing—books on passion and possibility, on the wisdom of myth, and the mystery of ancient initiation. Apparently she and I shared a fascination with ancient Egypt. More than that, here was someone who refused to be fettered by gender, a woman living life fully and out loud.

Free time was rare, but in 1993 I made the space for a ten-day workshop called "The Universal Human," up in Oregon. There were several classes available, taught by various luminaries. But I was only interested in meeting one teacher—Jean Houston.

I had just come back from a trip to Egypt. I not only felt a profound and powerful connection to the country (maybe I *was* once a Mesopotamian queen after all!) but I fell madly in love with their Egyptian goddess of healing, Sekhmet. Jean Houston had traveled to Egypt several times, and from her writing seemed equally smitten with their history and culture.

Right around this same time, Rosie had done a puzzling reading for me.

"Usually when I do a reading," she said afterward, "Spirit begins by addressing you as 'our beloved Kathy.' But this time, instead of 'Kathy,'

Spirit rattled off a bunch of other names." Rosie handed me a scribbled list, seven in all. Some of them I knew, like the Celtic goddess Brigid, but others were complete mysteries. I asked everyone I could think of for help in identifying them, from the WBA to members of the Transpersonal Psychology Institute. No one seemed to know who they were.

I had a hunch Jean might.

Before her lecture, I approached the dais, list in hand.

"You're Sicilian," she said—a statement, not a question—before I could open my mouth.

"How did you know?"

"Takes one to know one. I'm half-Sicilian myself." Indeed, we could have been sisters, except for our heights. (Jean is almost six feet tall, and I will always look up to her, in more ways than one!)

We traded genealogy for a minute. Then I handed over Rosie's list, along with a quick explanation.

"Is there anything you can tell me about these names?"

Jean scanned the column, her eyes widening.

"Ha!" she said, handing the paper back to me. "Well, looks like you're the triple goddess. Live with it." And she moved to the lectern to begin the class.

What the hell does that mean? I thought. Triple goddess, my foot.

Jean spoke eloquently and passionately about Isis and Osiris, and the importance of balancing feminine and masculine principles. She regaled us with tales of ancient Egypt. I lapped up her words.

When it was time for questions, I raised my hand. "Can you talk about Sekhmet?" I asked.

She cocked her head, and her eyes flashed. "Are you asking me that because of Robert?"

"Robert?"

"My husband Robert Masters. He wrote the foremost book about Sekhmet," Jean said.

I shook my head. I'd had no idea.

Later, Jean broke us into small groups for a more personal process. When she got to me, I had another question ready.

"What did you mean by triple goddess?"

Her eyes sparked again, with humor this time, but also immense power. "Well, Kathy, I don't want to scare you, but let me put it this way. You have a lot, A LOT, of archetypal entities around you. If I were you, I'd take that list of names seriously. Find out what they represent, and integrate their energy into your own."

I wondered if there was an *or else* attached.

"It will help you with your life's path," she said, much kinder than my own mind.

I'd never met anyone like this woman. I wanted whatever it was she had. How could I make her my friend?

At the time, I was helping organize the first Gorbachev State of the World Forum.

"How would you like to be a speaker?" I said, after a prolonged description. "I don't have any direct authority, but I'm working with the founders of the event."

"Sounds like fun," she said. And we exchanged information.

Shortly after the workshop, Jean was in Southern California on business. I invited her to my house. She plopped down in an easy chair in my living room, feet propped on the ottoman.

Jean Houston. Here in my house, relaxing on my armchair. A concrete demonstration of synchronicity, living breathing evidence that what you put out is what you get back.

"This is a wish come true," I said.

She arched her brows in question.

"Remember the Whole Life Expo in 1989? I was there at your lecture, sitting in the way back of the Hilton ballroom. You stepped on stage, and I said to myself *I must know this woman.*"

She offered an impish grin. "Welp, here I am," she said. "What do you want to know?"

We've been dear friends ever since, and yes, she feels like the sister I never had. We look alike. We laugh alike. Our voices even sound alike—although believe me, I wish I could speak like her! The woman uses twelve perfectly poetic adjectives in every sentence. Jean is a scholar, a philosopher and a pioneer of the human potential movement. She has traveled the world, studying ancient cultures, even working with the United Nations to transform educational models, in over one hundred countries. Her humility and humor mask a truly original and exceptionally brilliant mind.

Over the ensuing years, I've returned to Egypt with Jean, communing with Isis and Osiris. I've been to Bali, and Greece, diving deep into the roots of our world myths. Jean embodies the notion that every day counts and every moment offers a fresh opportunity to discover something transformational. (Jean was even responsible for my healthiest and most heart-opening romantic relationship—Paul and I met in Greece on a tour led by Jean.) I've learned and received so much from her! But spending time with Jean is as much about un-learning as it is about learning. She facilitates connecting with the divine at a very pure level—showing others how to dialogue with the higher self, and to practice personal empowerment.

"Take whatever is inside and use it! Cook on all burners," she loves to say to anyone willing to listen. "There's so much more within us all. Be fearless."

One day, we found ourselves talking over the issue of women helping other women. I'd confessed to her my corridor—the crowded hallway full of 'those that thirst.'

"I'm not even sure women like me all that much," I said. "How the heck am I supposed to feed them?"

Jean threw back her head and laughed, a full-throated crow of delight. Her laughter was liberating. Maybe I wasn't a traitor to the female race after all.

"I'm generally pretty happy when other women do well," I continued.

"But for whatever reason, for many women, with me, it's the opposite—it's as if my success makes them unhappy. I don't understand it."

"Maybe your strength *is* the problem," Jean said, her voice thoughtful. "Someone else's power can act as a reflection of our own weakness, a weakness we aren't even aware of. I've noticed this phenomenon as well. Too many women don't support other women, especially women in positions of power. It's a big problem." Her eyes grew dark and intense. I loved this warrior side of her. "This is the time for moving women forward. What are we waiting for? Kathy, the feminine energy is such a potent healing force!"

"I know," I said, my heart warming even more to this sister soul, who had impacted me so much already. "I know."

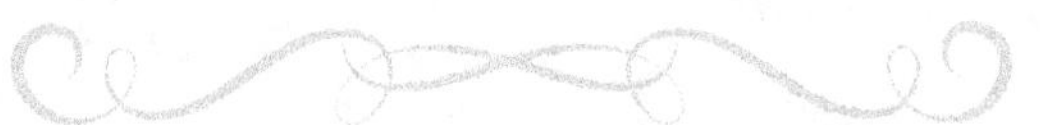

**The winds of grace are always blowing,
but it is you that must raise its sails.**

—RABINDRANATH TAGORE

Dear reader, if we want to thrive as women, we must *do the inner work*. It's the only path to true transformation. (It goes without saying this is also the case for men.) Self-confidence is not an attitude—it's an inside job first and foremost. As the singer Jewel once said, "I'm becoming more and more myself with time. I guess that's what grace is. The refinement of your soul over time."

Not everyone is ready to heal—and that goes for each and every one of us as well! The truth is, we can meet the wisest, most powerful person in the world, but unless we've addressed our own inner needs, we will never be open to change. How can we learn from someone whose strengths threaten us, shake our sense of self?

Only when I really and truly surrendered to the fact that I alone had to do the inner work, and everything started with inner acceptance, could I shift and grow. It's like a law of human nature. Do you feel deficient in some area? Guess what? You will see that lack in others. On the other hand, once we've found security within, we will not only feel happiness for others—what Buddhists call sympathetic joy—but like sound waves, the mutual joy amplifies, filling the surrounding space with positivity and healing.

An intuitive once told me, "You've come into this world to fly like an eagle. Along the way, there will be some broken-winged birds on the side of the road. You can stop and help them, but it could take you a lifetime. It may not be the highest and best use of your energy."

My body tells me the truth. If I feel drained, I know whatever I am hoping to do to help a situation, it's not working! I could stand on my head and wave my arms, shout at the top of my lungs, but no one's going to hear a word. I gently let go and move on. Otherwise, all I'm generating is frustration for others, and exhaustion for myself.

But if I stay grounded in love, I attract women and men who are open and curious. Their receptivity puts us both in a position to flower and to actually make a difference.

I've been on both sides of this equation. I've been resistant and receptive, close-fisted and openhearted. I've dug in my heels, and spread my wings.

How about you? Do you relate at all to resistance? Are you willing to do the inner work, and try something different?

I've discovered these simple, magical words when faced with another's success. "How wonderful for you! How did you do it?" My heart unlocks. Expressing appreciation and a willingness to learn and grow acts like a giant magnet for good things to come. When I celebrate the success of others, or offer to help them, or go the extra mile, I'm stunned at how quickly the universe responds by opening doors.

16

A New Set of Tools

**Modern femininity means having the
courage to explore ones own passion—
to live in the moment and refuse to s
eparate the beautiful from the everyday.**

—IPPOLITA ROSTAGNO

I moved homes once again, this time to a two-story house in South Laguna. My office—and our Qualis headquarters—was on the second floor, a spacious alcove at the top of the stairs with a big picture window overlooking the ocean. Leo's office was just down the hall.

One particularly challenging day, I pushed away from my desk in frustration. Nothing was going my way. I turned toward the window, my instinct when aggravated. My eyes were drawn to a dramatic *kerplash,* way in the distance—the distinctive signal of a breeching whale.

I took it as a sign.

"Leo," I called. "Let's go chase a whale!"

Soon he was steering our boat into the bay, with me as his crew and compass. By the time we reached our goal, there wasn't a single whale to be found. The sky had grown overcast, and my mood followed suit, plummeting.

"Great," I grumbled. "One more disappointment."

No sooner had I spoken these words than a pod of dolphins drew beside our hull. They surrounded our boat, leaping and frolicking, a physical manifestation of pure joy. Leo and I laughed along with them, and soon my heart lifted and danced as well. They'd sent me a message I would not forget—it's okay to play, Kathy. In fact, it's necessary! I returned home refreshed and renewed.

I'd transferred the soul painting to my new bedroom wall. Still no features, not yet. But my relationship with my soul's purpose was getting warmer.

Every day offered another opportunity to use a new set of tools, and they weren't all about forcefulness, either. I was learning how to receive as well as give—to be yielding as well as strong. As I started to find my own stride—a rhythm and pace that suited me—I continued to refine a dress code all my own.

There were very few executive women in the workplace when I started out. We were like a rare breed of bird, with no set plumage. Mostly, women were encouraged to dress like men, the better to blend into the crowd. Business suits for women were shapeless and somber, black or gray with an occasional pinstripe. Blouses came with built-in ties.

In another corner was the frilly mode of dress for the little woman at home—pastel prettiness decorated with ruffles and charm.

And finally there were clothes for the seductive siren, the forbidden fruit. Fashion for women who chose—or were forced to choose—to dress like attention-getting magnets.

None of these options suited me. I've always loved fabric, fashion, and jewelry—the variety of design and color, the range of textures. Yes, I spent most of my time in the workplace, but I wasn't about to dress like men just because I spent most of my time with them. I found myself drawn to jeweled hues, royal purples and dark blues and greens—the colors of amethysts and sapphires and emeralds. I furnished my home with textured wallpapers and upholstered furniture in bronze and copper tones. My closet was like a treasure chest, and lifted my spirits every morning.

I only bought what I loved—quality, not quantity. Dresses that flowed, blouses that wrapped, but never too short or too low cut—if you're the only woman on a work site, why invite unwanted attention? I dressed to please myself, without becoming a distraction to others. (I'd been to more than a few meetings by then where a woman's unskilled clothing choice skewed the whole room.) I was also grateful for my dark brown hair. Sadly, it was an energetic advantage not to be a blonde in the business world.

One day, I passed an Escada store—so out of reach growing up it might as well have been Antarctica. A suit hanging in the window caught my eye—a rich, vibrant purple, with white piping.

Why not?

They had my size. I tried it on in the elegant Escada dressing room, and quickly discovered the skirt bunched and the jacket hung oddly. I'd already checked the price tag, so I wasn't exactly heartbroken. Still, the color was breathtaking. A saleswoman stepped beside me as I turned and twisted in front of a full-length mirror.

"Don't worry," she said. "We have a wonderful seamstress who can help you."

That's how I met the marvelous Hilda. She walked into the dressing room and stared at me as if she already knew me. I felt the same—it was 'like at first sight.'

"You are of Italian descent, yes?" she asked as she tugged at the skirt. Her eastern-European accent was exotic—Turkish, I would later learn.

"Yes."

"This is good color for you. You should always wear deep color like this." She pinned and tucked until the suit miraculously fit. "If you come back in a week, I will have ready for you."

The following week, she slipped me her personal card along with the finished suit.

"I want to sew for you in my home," she said.

I soon learned the story behind her fashion wizardry. Hilda was born in Istanbul, but learned *haute couture* in France. She eventually made her way to Orange County, and soon was sewing for women of taste and means up and down the coast. But as far as I know, I am one of only a few clients she's invited into her home!

The steep price of that purple suit was worth every penny even though it hangs untouched in my closet to this day, never worn, tag still dangling. I keep it not as a cautionary tale, nor as physical evidence that I own Escada. I keep it as an emblem of gratitude for bringing Hilda into my life. Because of her, wherever I travel, I take the time to find the local fabric-makers. Every culture has its own costume, and I love to bring home bolts of cloth that call to me from every corner of the world, so that Hilda can turn the raw material into wearable art. She and I still work together in this way, every hand-sewn piece a testament to the pleasure and power of co-creating. Whenever I put on one of her inspired inventions, I feel wrapped in love.

My affection for fashion did not go unnoticed among my peers. During this time, the chairman of the World Business Academy, George McCown, became a close friend. His venture capital firm bought Vans Shoe Company in the early 1990's and he'd skillfully shepherded it out of bankruptcy. Like many NASDEQ companies at the time, there were no women on the Vans Board of Directors. One day George pulled me aside to ask if I'd consider joining.

"Why?" I asked. "I know nothing about sports shoes. I mean, have you seen what I wear on my feet?" I motioned with one three-inch heel.

"Ah, but you know the worlds of fashion *and* distribution," George said. "Vans is branching out. They're developing a new program called 'The Ageless Woman.' I'm thinking you can help out with design ideas."

I didn't know about becoming the poster girl for The Ageless

Woman, but I loved the idea of working with George. I said yes. As an added bonus, Vans was located in Southern California, so meetings would be easy to attend.

At my first Vans board meeting, sure enough, a nice big poster proclaiming the new Ageless Woman line was affixed to the door.

Never to be seen again, unfortunately.

Every three months I'd pick George up at the John Wayne Airport in Orange County and ferry him to the quarterly daylong meetings. We'd start at nine in the morning. By four o'clock, when we adjourned, I would limp out the door with a splitting headache. I never got headaches, so for me this was a new, and unwelcome phenomenon.

By the third headache, I'd had enough. I brought up my concerns with George on our way back to the airport.

"That board is pretty intense," I said, my temples throbbing. "There's a whole lot of ego-banging going on in the room, you know? They're manufacturing some kind of potent male energy-field, for sure."

He nodded, as if in agreement, so I plowed ahead.

"I'm not sure I'm adding much, Ageless Woman or not."

"About that…" George glanced sideways at me. "I may not have been completely straight with you. I didn't invite you on the board to talk about fashion. I invited you because, as you just pointed out, we desperately need some feminine energy in the room. I've seen how you work. There's nobody better."

Great. Another call to be a flipping fountain.

I knew one thing for sure—I couldn't address the boardroom dynamics without being centered and in balance myself.

I regrouped. Acute cranial pain is not conducive to emitting positive energy. If I were going to survive, I would need to change direction and apply my "David" strategy to this new cause. I was actually curious to see if beaming unconditional love could work on a group level. At the same time, I knew from experience that I needed to come from a position of strength and self-protection. The solution, as always, started with me.

Before every board meeting, I would settle into my heart area and let it remind me why I was there.

Not to "win against," but to "add to."

Not to have the loudest voice in the room, but to be of service to the greater good.

Not to judge, but to lead with love.

These were all brilliant men—mathematically astute and economically intelligent and they knew merchandising inside and out. But time and again, as the comments flew, their linear approach would lead to a struggle for power. This brand of competition limited problem-solving, and blocked the path to solutions.

I'd raise my hand whenever I sensed a narrowing of perspective. "What about the employees?" I'd ask. And, "How does this change affect customers?" And, "Shouldn't we consider the big picture?" I spoke without rancor, grounded in a place of absolute acceptance of what everyone in the room was, and wasn't. We were all tiny slivers of the same divine light, and I communicated from that spirit-based place of conviction—my higher self, reaching out to theirs.

It was like magic. The entire energy field would shift, like a weather system changing before my eyes. Bodies relaxed. The conversation became solution-based, win-win instead of victory at any cost.

Even I was shocked at the power of this practice. To be able to sit quietly and change the field of energy so that it supported resolution? What a secret weapon!

I was the only woman on the Vans board for seven of the ten years I served, and stayed on until the company was sold. It was a transformational experience for me as well. Gone were the headaches. In their place was the opportunity to grow in business acumen and conscious commerce. As a public company Vans, unlike Qualis, had to deal with Wall Street and shareholders and I loved learning about a different model of accountability. I also got to practice a new way of being. It was a redo of the Five Guys experience. I stayed put, and stayed grounded. I not only didn't lose myself in the process, I grew in stature. I might still be the only skirt in the room, but this time I claimed my chair, not only as an equal, but an additive presence.

In a way, my career has been one long lesson in irony. I left the Five Guys to become the rep for a number of new clients, but it soon became clear that the Home Depot was my main account. The faster the Depot grew, the more time they demanded of me. Soon, I found myself in an all-too-familiar position, the lone female navigating an alien world, only this one was populated top to bottom with lifetime members of the tool-belt crowd. None of them cared one whit about higher states of consciousness or spiritual practices.

Which turned out to be fine. Their path was none of my business, and I stopped expecting my corporate clients to share my point of view. But my calling hadn't changed, not since that first soul painting. My mission was to *be* the values that I held. The rest would take care of itself.

While women CEO's were still the minority, more and more started joining the world of business. All were hard-working and determined. All were exhausted. And after a while I discovered all were dogged by the same question—can we have it all? Can we work toward a fulfilling career, marry, have children, and maintain some kind of balance without losing our minds, our health, or our souls?

In some ways, the query itself assumes a level of comfort that is belied by the hardcore reality of much of the world. This difficult truth was brought home to me—forceful as an awakening slap—during the third annual Gorbachev State of the World Forum. I thought I was well versed in the personal challenges of working women, the dilemmas inherent in raising children while building a career. Yes, for years I was a single mother, and yes, I was working twelve-hour days, juggling responsibilities like a circus clown. I'd always assumed I knew what it was to struggle, especially when I fell into bed every night, asleep before my head hit the pillow.

Then I heard Muhammed Yunus speak.

This life-changing opportunity arrived, like so many others, as a result of the World Business Academy. In 1991, Mikhail Gorbachev stepped down from his position as President of the USSR. A year later, the Gorbachev Foundation opened its doors, his dream child and an institution dedicated to promoting "democratic values as well as moral and humanist principles in the life of society." The foundation put forth the idea that massive globalization required a new way of thinking and being, via transformational ideas and principles, and greater humanism and equity worldwide. This call for change from across the world echoed our own academy's mission.

Gorbachev reached out to the brilliant theologian and futurist Jim Garrison that same year to found a North American branch of the Gorbachev Foundation. Garrison's job was to develop programs that reflected the foundation's commitment to far-reaching humanistic ideals.

Who better to brainstorm with in this regard than Rinaldo Brutoco, the president of the World Business Academy? It helped that Jim and Rinaldo were already friends. Together, they cooked up the timely idea of holding an annual Gorbachev State of the World Forum. The idea was to hold these events annually up to and including the birth of the next millennium, ushering in a new century by suggesting new models for change. These weeklong events, staged in San Francisco, would bring together Gorbachev and other world leaders using a round table format. Like King Arthur and his knights, world leaders of every race and gender would come together to discuss subjects ranging from technology, to world hunger, to globalization, to everything else under the sun. During each forum, one or two general plenary sessions would be open to the public, and include fascinating speakers from all over the world.

Rinaldo called with yet another life-changing invitation. "Kathy, you'll love this group. You have to get involved."

I was thrilled to contribute. I reached out to Jean first, and she was soon a featured participant, even delivering the closing speech in Grace Cathedral one year. I contacted my favorite poet, David Whyte, and he became the forum's lyrical voice, opening and ending each session and meal with a heart-opening poem.

The first forum took place in late September, 1995. Over 400 leaders and thinkers from at least fifty countries convened. Physicists and cellists, priests and poets, business executives and anthropologists, humanitarians and politicians, all debated the way forward for humanity in a post-Cold War world.

And the forum kept evolving. We looked around that first year, and realized that diversity was sorely lacking. Over the next several years we included the very young and the very old, more women, more people of color. Everyone's opinion was welcomed, every point of view heard. We discovered that greater diversity led to greater creativity—as author and educational pioneer Nancy Kline puts it, "Diversity raises the intelligence of groups." Soon we had one hundred and one different nations and tribes represented. We filled ballrooms, a thousand people at a time.

Year two, I was seated at a table during one dinner session, chatting away with a group of friends from the academy. A man stepped onto the stage, skin like cocoa, with bright eyes and a warm smile. His simple Nehru tunic covered loose cotton pants. He was short in stature but his presence filled the room.

"I am Muhammed Yunus," he said. "I come from Bangladesh."

He described his amazing path—his acquisition of a PhD in economics in America, his return to Bangladesh to teach economics at a university there, and his moment of moral clarity. How one day he realized that he left the university grounds every afternoon after teaching the privileged few, only to step straight into abject poverty for the many.

He decided to take his students on a field trip, to visit the villages surrounding the university and see how economics translated into actual life.

In one local village, he and his students discovered a group of women fashioning chairs and stools out of bamboo—handmade furniture that was both beautiful, and functional.

"These are wonderful," he commented. "You must make a lot of money selling your wares in the marketplace."

The women hooted. "A lot of money?" one said. "We make one *taka*."

Muhammed paused in his story and addressed us directly, a room full of rapt listeners. "In case you're wondering, that's the equivalent of a single penny," he said.

"How can that be?" he asked the women. Well, they told him, a man from the city bought all the bamboo himself and delivered it to them, for a price they couldn't possibly pay, putting them in debt. They earned a penny for every stool they made, an amount that barely put a dent in the amount they owed.

Muhammed's mind started calculating. "How much is the bamboo?" he asked.

Twenty cents per chair, they told him, twenty-five for the better quality.

And what if you were to buy your own bamboo and sell the stools and chairs at the marketplace yourself, would that be of interest?

Why yes, it certainly would, but who would do that for us? We need a lot of bamboo and we have no money to buy it.

Muhammed pressed further—were other women in other villages falling into debt, making furniture for a penny a chair?

Yes, they were.

He found ten such villages to begin with. Then he paid a visit to the local bank.

The banker scoffed. "These are poor people, and women besides," he said. "A terrible loan risk. You'll see, they'll never pay you back."

Muhammed returned to the villages.

"How much would it take for you to make a start?" he asked.

The answer was twenty-seven dollars. Twenty-seven dollars, to buy enough bamboo to make enough products to sell at enough profit to reinvest.

Muhammed fronted them the seed money. They quickly paid him back. He found more women to support. *They* paid him back.

Ten villages became twenty became one hundred, and finally Muhammed returned to the bank with columns of numbers.

"Look," he said. "It's working. They are paying their debt and growing their business."

"It's a fluke," the bank manager replied. "These are poor people, and women besides. Your model is not sustainable."

So Muhammed Yunus opened his own bank.

He looked across the crowded ballroom where we sat, still spellbound.

"I'm not a banker! I'm an economics teacher!" he said. "But our bank just funded our first billion in loans. We've never had a late payment, not once, and 95% of our loans are with women. The model *is* sustainable, and not just in Bangladesh. All across the globe, in impoverished nations, women are starting these micro-businesses, and families are growing stronger and healthier. When you empower women, the whole family is empowered—the good trickles down."

In my case, it was tears trickling down.

My dinner mate nudged me. "You're so emotional," he said.

"Are you kidding?" I replied. "All the times I've wasted twenty-seven dollars buying nothing, and here this man used the same amount to put a whole village of women into business?"

His greater goal was to end poverty in the world, and he didn't just talk about it, he took substantive action. Many countries have used his model to raise the standard of living in their poorest communities. He is a true inspiration to me. And I never looked at twenty-seven dollars the same way again.

Muhammed Yunus, Marilyn Ferguson, Thich Nat Han, Jane Goodall, and a host of other pioneers for humanity who attended these World Forums broadened my horizons, deepened my understanding, and offered glimpses into worlds I'd otherwise never know existed. Quite the education!

Still, each of us has to start where we are, and build from there. And those of us fortunate enough to live in this land of plenty still have wants, and hopes, and dreams.

Which brings me back to that pesky question, achingly familiar to women the world over. Can we have it all?

I was fully engaged in my work, surrounded by friends, my son by my side. I held my feet to the fires of love and purpose every day to grow my business and my life, and be of service to spirit. All that I lacked was a partner, someone with whom I could celebrate all these new experiences. A person to share my joys, as well as my sorrows.

One afternoon I found myself bemoaning that lack at great length with a friend, as we awaited a delayed flight out of San Francisco. Jerry had long receded in the distance of my rearview mirror, but no one had yet come close to replacing him.

"Here's what you should do," my dear friend Karen McCown said. "Make a list of everything you really want in a man, the things you have to have in a partner."

"You mean, like a wish list?"

"Exactly. Come on, let's do it right now!"

We moved to a corner of the waiting area and I dutifully pulled a notebook from my briefcase."

My pen hovered. I glanced at her. "I don't know what to write. I actually have no idea."

"Just jot down all the things you've gotta have," Karen said. "Don't think about it too hard."

"Okay."

Good legs, I wrote. (I know, I know, but that's what came up for me first.)

Sense of humor
Emotional Intelligence
Successful in business
Likes to travel

The list swelled until it covered three pages. I was shocked. I guess I did have a bunch of specific wants after all. Finally I put my pen down.

"Now what?" I asked Karen.

She skimmed my list. "Okay, a lot of these are duplicates. See if you can get it down to one page. Then transfer the list onto a piece of beautiful stationary and carry it with you wherever you go.

So that's what I did.

Every new date, every blossoming relationship, I would surreptitiously run my mind down the list. This one has a sense of humor, but didn't like to travel. That one was enormously successful, but fairly insensitive. One man was both brilliant and artistic, and his home housed a collection of art worthy of a museum. I could sense the little boy deep within him, but the barricade between his mind and his heart was impenetrable, and not mine to breach. No one matched the list. I would always start out hopeful, but eventually move on.

Meanwhile, Qualis was thriving, and so was I.

It was time for a second soul painting. This time, I would sit in the same room with Rosie as she let the image unfold.

"I'd better have a face this time," I told her, settling into a chair across from the easel.

Rosie's breathing slowed. She became as still as stone.

I waited.

She plucked a brush and dipped it into a small pot of blue paint.

I could barely breathe.

Suddenly she was off and running, paintbrush flying. I had to force myself not to walk behind her and peek at the work in progress.

Please let me have features, please let me have features.

"It is finished," Rosie finally murmured. The twenty minutes had felt like a lifetime, and like no time at all.

She turned the canvas my way. A smile swept across my face.

The figure before me had two eyes, a nose, and a mysterious smile. Her expression hinted at both humor and wisdom. The features were soft, but also strong—a wonderful balance of masculine and feminine energies. All around this powerful figure an intense light radiated, as if the body itself was armored with rays of love.

"Does this mean I don't have to feed the thirsty any longer?" I asked, ever hopeful.

Rosie's smile was patient.

"No, dear," she said. "It means you're finally ready to start."

Great. So that was still going to be a thing.

"By the way," Rosie added, "I did a reading on you and relationships recently. Spirit had a lot to say."

"Oh good," I answered, "because I made my own list of what I want in a partner. Let's compare!"

I pulled out the thick sheet of cream-colored vellum and unfolded it. Glancing at the top item, I paused.

"You, first," I said.

Rosie closed her eyes, and if recalling an inner inventory. "Spirit asks you this—Can you love another without judgment? Can you not lose yourself in the relationship? Can you stand on your own two feet and hold yourself to your own highest spiritual standard? Can you stay true to your life's purpose, while committed to another in love?

Oh.

She reached for my list.

"No way," I said, folding it back up.

"Kathy…"

"Okay, fine, but don't judge me." I passed it over reluctantly.

"Good legs?" Rosie read, her voice quizzical. She threw back her head and laughed.

"What?" My face was flushed. "I can't have that?"

"Of course you can," she said. "But maybe don't make it number one on the list, okay?"

When I got home, I hung the second soul painting below the first one.

As I gazed at the two portraits of spirit, a thought hit me.

Nothing was actually lacking in my life.

And if that was true, why was I making a list identifying the things I needed? All that did was empower a sense of lack. So I made another list, shorter and sweeter. I started at the top with a brand new item, more invitation than expression of want.

I welcome in someone with whom I can feel completely authentic, fearless and free to pursue my life's purpose and passion.

Below that I added, *I welcome in his good legs.*

**To bring anything into your life,
imagine that it is already there.**

—RICHARD BACH

Dear reader, we already have everything we need. Once we understand this profound truth, we can *change wanting into welcoming in.* This simple concept can be such a powerful tool. It's like the practice of gratitude—it shifts everything!

Wanting has its roots in lack and fear. It wears the heavy crown of the victim, and sits on a throne of discontent.

Welcoming in floats in an ocean of abundance. It accepts the notion that the universe is both generous and benevolent.

So have courage, dear reader. Knowing this, welcome in your wildest dreams. Then fasten your seatbelt, and get ready for the rocket ride of your life!

17

WHERE I CHOOSE TO LIVE

**Happiness is when what you think, what you say,
and what you do are in harmony.**

—MAHATMA GANDHI

The undeveloped hillside had beckoned like a promise for years. It sat high on its throne over the Pacific, serene yet alluring, wearing a fringe of pampas grass. I would drive by the untamed point of land every day and think, There's a place to build a home—beautiful, peaceful, and out of the fray.

Finally, the Irvine Company pitched a sales tent at the top of Pelican Point, and hired architects to design model homes, jewels that would suit this magnificent setting.

Like a sea bird, I had circled this very spot for most of my life. Manhattan Beach, Playa Del Rey, Huntington Beach, Lake Forest, Newport Beach, South Laguna—wherever I landed I was never far from the ocean. But now it was time to build a home from the foundation upward, a place that truly reflected what I had learned, and who I wanted to be.

I perused the builders' choices, and was instantly drawn to one of four potential designs. It was instant attraction, but only on paper. I signed up for a home based on a blueprint. The reality was well over a year from completion.

The Irvine Company had planned the development of Crystal Cove meticulously. Finding the right owners for these initial houses was Phase One.

"How many homes are you actually building during the first phase?" I asked.

"Six. Three models, two on each block."

"And how many names on the list?"

"One hundred."

"So how do I add mine?"

They told me to identify the model I wanted—that part was easy—and then to choose the lot I preferred.

I invited my friend Fred to walk the two possibilities with me. He had a good eye, and he knew architecture.

The first lot had room for a large back yard, and was closer to the golf course and the harbor. I thought it might be a preferable location.

We moved on to bachelor number two, Lot 29.

This space was completely unpaved, and we crunched our way up a graded and dusty dirt rise. At the top was an enormous cavernous hole, surrounded by an orange fence so people like me wouldn't tumble in accidentally.

Fred was fascinated by the mysterious and massive excavation. "What in the world?" He sniffed around its perimeter, looking for clues as to its purpose.

I was drawn to the view beyond. At the top of the graded slope, I paused. I caught my breath. Off in the distance, the ocean and sky met like lovers, interchanging light and cloud in a constant dance before my eyes. As I inhaled the faint hint of salty air, I was reminded of my first glimpse of the ocean, decades ago.

It smelled like freedom.

A small flutter hooked the edge of my attention, and I turned to look. The construction site was pristine, but the workers must have missed this—a strip of plastic half-buried in the dirt. I wandered over to investigate.

And saw the Qualis logo—a pyramid-shaped Q—waving, as if staking a claim to this piece of land. What in the world?

I leaned closer. The torn remnant of a Home Depot bag had somehow been overlooked in the nightly cleanup, and my company logo riffled in the breeze like a banner. I'd chosen the pyramid to represent both soul and success—head in the sky, feet firmly on the ground. Qualis as I wanted it to be, a marriage between spirit and business, making heaven earthbound.

Welcome home, the fluttering logo now seemed to say.

Fred was still trying to figure out the underground cave—we would later learn it was for a subterranean wine cellar, one of only seven in the entire Crystal Cove development.

"Fred! Come look!" I said.

He joined me, and started to laugh. "God planted a flag for you," he said.

"I know," I murmured. "This is the one, isn't it?" I plucked the scrap of plastic and tucked it into my purse.

I put my name down for both lots, just in case. I knew the chances were slim either way. I wasn't in control, but if ever there was a wink from the universe…

Still, if I've learned anything from a lifetime in business, it's that footwork helps, but relationships are everything. As a single woman buyer, I needed to dot all my i's. I had my bank send a letter showing that I qualified for the loan. I also made sure to lead with love—making friends with the Irvine Company salespeople, bringing them flowers and cupcakes, learning about their lives. I dropped in frequently, never empty-handed, always openhearted. They had one hundred applicants for six slots, but I had to believe they were also looking for people they liked who would attract other people they liked.

Months later I was on the phone with my friends Amy and Monte in New York, a wonderful couple who also happen to be tremendously gifted at Tarot readings. They've built a successful business because of this gift. I told them about the six lots, and the list of one hundred potential buyers.

"Let's do a reading," Monte said.

"No!" I said. "I don't want to jinx it!"

"I've already laid out the cards," he replied.

"C'mon. Ask a question," Amy chimed in over the phone.

With Tarot readings, the cards don't tell you yes or no, only if something is favorable. "Okay. Am I going to get a lot at Crystal Cove?"

"It's favorable," Monte answered after a moment.

Encouraged, I tried a second question. "I signed up for two lots. So…is it the lot closer to the golf course?"

"Nope. The other one." Monte said.

"The cards are pretty emphatic," Amy added.

So was my heart.

A week later, I got the call. "

"Lot 29 is yours if you want it," the saleswoman said.

"Sold," I said.

That was in 2001, thirteen short years since I started Qualis International. That simple act of faith that took every ounce of courage I had, and led me literally to this beautiful home on a hill.

Qualis has thrived not because I knew what I was doing, but because I dared to lead with love. Over almost three decades of existence, we have never experienced a lawsuit, or undercut a client, or left a problem unsolved. As a company, we pride ourselves in taking 100% responsibility for every aspect of our business.

We were vendors for Home Depot for thirty years—unheard of in our world. And after twenty years in business together, the Home

Depot diversity department held a big event at the downtown Los Angeles Bonaventure to honor Qualis—along with nine other women-owned businesses serving as vendors and suppliers. Together, we had changed a deep-seated culture of patriarchy.

All our staffs were invited. The Depot presented Qualis with an engraved crystal plaque and our own personal star in the universe—a heartfelt tribute to a woman-owned company that produced over thirty million dollars a year.

That's right. Qualis has its own star in the constellation Scorpius, registered in both Switzerland and Washington D.C. as "The Home Depot Salutes Qualis." Imagine that—written forever in the cosmos!

When you consider I almost left the account, you can see why I believe anything is possible. (And by the way, Abdullah turned out to be right. My name is on three corporations today, Qualis International plus two LLCs.)

Anne Frank once said, "Everyone has inside of him a piece of good news. The good news is that you don't know how great you can be! How much you can love! How much you can accomplish! And what your potential is!"

Qualis turned out to be the single greatest vehicle for my personal, professional, and spiritual growth. Because of my company's success, I was finally able to choose how I wanted to live.

I planted two giant palms at the top of the ridge overlooking the ocean. Osiris stands where the Qualis logo once fluttered. His partner Isis looms a few feet to his right. Their roots reach deep underground, crisscrossing the earth to form a safe cradle of masculine and feminine strength.

"Come see," I said to Jean, the first time she came to visit. I hurried her to the outside terrace and pointed to the lofty palms.

"You'll never guess in a million years what their names are."

"Isis and Osiris," Jean said, without batting an eye.

Inside my home, this balance between masculine and feminine is replicated in every room. I am surrounded with layered meaning, the bitter and the sweet, the darkness and the light, the *he* and the *she* of things. For every object that strengthens my spine, another opens my heart. For every photo of someone long gone, there's another of a newfound friend.

I like it that way. As Osho once said, "Sadness gives roots. Happiness gives branches. Both are needed."

My home is filled with reminders that sometimes I need to lead, and other times to lean. Sometimes steer, and other times, let go.

Upstairs on a side table, *Kuan Yin* stands with proffered urn, reminding me to practice kindness and compassion. Across from her hangs a painting of a goddess, sitting on a bed of lotus flowers, holding the universe in the form of a crystal—holding space for peace and love in the world. Be truthful, they both seem to say, echoing Gandhi. Be gentle. Be fearless.

The reclining Buddha's enigmatic smile greets me as I pass him every day. Wise and compassionate, he reminds me that with our thoughts, we make the world.

Every Christmas I bring out my hand-crafted elves, Zeke and Oliver, their pointed velvet shoes and rakish grins a saucy reminder to be generous, to take joy where we can, and to spread good will to all.

Smiling photographs decorate every table—so many framed moments of friendship and love with dear friends like Deepak and Jean, with my son Leo and my granddaughter Alyssa, as miraculous to me now as the day she arrived. I held her in my arms and was struck by the utter innocence of her newborn soul.

I looked over at Leo and said, "She doesn't know to hate. Our job is just to teach her love."

Love.

Next to my favorite armchair sits a magnificent white quartz crystal, tall and multi-faceted, belonging to my late love and dearest partner Paul. It lights up from the inside. The crystal lived at Paul's house for years—his most beloved possession, next to me. Paul would point to its inner glow whenever I got flustered or impatient.

"Remember, Kathy, only love is real," Paul would say. "The rest is white noise."

Paul showed up in Greece—a fellow traveler following Jean Houston's lead, and it was Jean who first pointed out his assets. I was no longer actively seeking a partner—I was very happy and fulfilled with or without a Soul mate. It turns out that's the perfect time to find one. Emotional intelligence? Check. Loves to travel? Check. Successful in business, sense of humor, comfortable in his own skin? Check, check, check.

Added bonuses—he loved to cook, could fix just about anything that was broken, and yes, he had great legs.

Most of all, his spiritual path was as primary to him as mine was to me.

Our time together was far too short, but I wouldn't trade a minute of it. He taught me to trust, to open my heart. Because of Paul, I choose to believe our souls are spacious enough to handle more than one mate in our lifetime.

Upstairs, my library houses a treasure trove of books, some by dear friends, others by strangers I'd want for friends were I lucky enough to meet them. Books about inner discovery and outer travel. Poetry books for the soul, and cookbooks for the stomach. (If you want a recipe for real *Pasta e Fagioli*, no cans involved, just ask!)

The painting by the wife of my late navy SEAL friend Mike Blondell guards the hallway, encouraging me to keep walking my spiritual path.

A gift that came from him, through her.

Isis and Osiris, masculine and feminine, *yin* and *yang*, everywhere I look.

And just outside my bedroom hang Rosie's two soul paintings, one above the other. The first came to me at a time when I was still trying to find my way—the colors are muted, the forms indistinct. But I no longer view it with dread. The central form looks stronger and more grounded. If she has actual features, they still have yet to rise to the surface, but who's to say that's wrong? This way, she's whoever I want her to be at any given moment!

Below her, my second soul painting radiates color, purpose, and power. You can just make out in the lower left hand corner the image of a man, supportive where he rests. Spirit told Rosie this masculine being has been with me many times before, and will be with me again in the future.

For years I thought it was a yet-to-be-discovered mate. Then I decided it was my son.

Now I don't think it's either.

I think it's another aspect of me.

For my 60th birthday, I invited dear friends to celebrate with me in Las Vegas—who says spiritual has to mean staid? Jean Houston put on quite a show, channeling my 200-year-old Italian great-grand-mother, who apparently had lots of sage if bawdy advice for me, direct from the ether.

David and his wife flew out for the party. He stood up at the mic and made quite the illuminating toast, alluding to how difficult I was to work with at first.

"We used to have these screaming matches," he said. "I wasn't sure I could keep doing business with her!"

My fellow WBA members laughed quietly on the other side of the ballroom.

"But ya know what?" David finished. "I love Kathy. Qualis is the best company anyone could ever work with." We all drank to that.

At my latest birthday milestone, one of my oldest and dearest friends from the Academy, Jim Cusumano, flew to Newport Beach from Prague to help me celebrate. This lovely man has worn more wildly successful career hats than I can count, from entrepreneur, to hotelier, to author, to physicist, to hit songwriter and singer in a popular 1950's boy band.

After dinner, Jim put on a rocking half-hour show. We danced and cheered as he serenaded us with song after song from my teenage years. For the finale, Jim invited my girlfriend and me up on the stage to be his back-up singers. He launched into his very first hit song.

"Who wears short-shorts?" he sang.

"*We* wear short-shorts!" we crowed.

What can I say? Peak experiences come in many forms.

I'm less day-to-day with the business now, content to let my son do most of the driving. Leo has always been calmer than me. He instinctively embodies both Osiris and Isis as he shepherds our company into the future. Qualis is in safe hands.

My mother is going strong as well. She and I are still worlds apart at times, but we are stitched close by love in all the ways that matter.

Like nesting dolls, all these earlier Kathy's are still inside me. The perfectionist and the rebel. The girl at the altar and the woman in the business suit. The Mesopotamian queen and the dental receptionist with a toddler at her knees. The only difference is, the container is more spacious today. There is enough room, and enough love, for all of me. I'm not an angel yet—but who knows?

Maybe one day I'll wake up and those fountains will have finally turned into wings.

Nature is based on harmony.

—Bruce Lipton

Dear reader, for me, spirit and success could only coexist when I learned to *balance masculine and feminine energies.*

This applies to both women and men, by the way! As my friend Jim Cusumano says, "We are all born with both energies, and the cultural hypnosis of our society instructs—no, brainwashes!—us how and when to use each."

When I was fed up with the five guys, I was really angry, and set out to prove that a woman could have and run a company. I couldn't bear the injustice, the unfairness around women in business. I charged ahead, with fierce determination. Anger and ambition served me well at the time.

The truth is, I've always had a lot of male energy, and for much of my life I've primarily lived in that field.

I also love being a woman. I love the creative, confident female energy, and given a choice, I even prefer to live there! But whenever there were problems or situations that needed solving, whenever my back was against the wall, I would ALWAYS resort to relying on my masculine energy. Over time, it began to wear me out.

I am so curious—how have these two energies played out in you?

I've come to believe that all of us need to honor and embody both male and female energy to stay in balance, to use all of what we are. I've stopped making either one right or wrong—done with integrity and love, both approaches are a divine way to be.

The benefits of balancing the masculine and feminine in business are clear. As for finding the right balance with a life partner, here, too, this is a huge issue. That impulse within all of us to do what we came here to do can be so strong, yet we don't always choose a partner who supports that. Look at me! When I was out in the world, I was fine. Whenever I joined my partner after work, I would shrink. I made myself less so he could be more.

I'm sure I'm not the first person to experience this.

I reached the point where I had to adjust my priorities. Dear reader, I've accepted this truth for years now—my spiritual path down my particular hallway comes first. It's number one.

Once I made my soul's purpose central, the right man came into my life—someone who could be Osiris to my Isis, and Isis to my Osiris. I discovered with Paul that having a partner with equal spiritual passion was not only possible, but preferable! He taught me that in relationships, too, unconditional love reinforces wholeness and healing. And when he died after only three years together, my heart had learned enough to break, before breaking wide open, making room for even more light to come in.

Only love is real. The rest is white noise.

Be the Change

**Everything is what it is.
And then, it will be what you make it.**

—PAT SUMMIT

Dear reader, I have so enjoyed spending this time with you! Putting down these snapshots of my life has been a joy and a revelation.

Working for thirty years with Home Depot gave me an appreciation for tools, how the right tool at the right time can make any challenge easier. And so I've tried to offer you mine, transformational tools honed over time, grounded in feminine principles. I've relied on the personal, in the hopes that my stories may also prove practical.

This is truly a time of moving women forward. We must hold our feet to the fire. Strive to spend more time living in the awareness of love, and not allowing our linear thoughts to rule our actions. We must choose to be vigilant in our efforts to create a more loving environment in business. The balanced feminine energy is so needed right now, and courageous women can use their genius and passion to transform businesses into powerful centers of value for the greater good. If we gather together and use our collective field of intelligence, we can help each other unlock the potential we all hold.

We are all here to learn how to love.

Love and service elevates our soul. And connecting the head with the heart is the most important thing we can do in business, not to mention in life!

Corporate transformation can only occur through personal transformation. Those of us on a spiritual path are called to be the architects of this transformation, and we must hold ourselves 100% responsible for the way we do business. But leading with confidence, compassion, right action, and clarity? It's always an inside job first, my friend.

Always.

I invite you to join me, as together we hold our feet to the fire—the fire of unconditional love, the fire of radical change, the fire that will light the future and surround all our successes with spirit.

The Latin word for spirit, *spiritus*, is also the word for breathe. Let's all take a deep breath, and go out and live our dreams!

Thank you so much for this privilege of sharing my heart with you.

Beyond our ideas of right-doing
and wrong-doing there is a field.

I'll meet you there.

—JALALUDDIN RUMI

Tools for Transformation

Thank God our time is now when wrong
Comes up to face us everywhere,
Never to leave us till we take
The longest stride of soul we ever took.

—CHRISTOPHER FRY

1. **Know your early drivers.** Success is an inside job. We won't heal or evolve unless and until we are willing to shine a light on our hidden motivators, to really examine them. Remember, you can't give what you don't have.

2. **Question inherited beliefs.** Look for where they do or don't resonate, using intuition like a divining rod. Keep whatever works, and let go of the rest, with gratitude.

3. **Go where the love is.** Everyone deserves accolades and acceptance. We are all born in light, and worthy of love. Seek loving mentors—they are waiting to be found.

4. **Know thyself.** We must learn to look inside, to explore and accept our own deepest needs and beliefs. Only then, can we meet others on equal ground.

5. **Recognize dysfunctional systems.** Learn to gaze with unblinking eyes on the personal and cultural ideas that serve as our incubators. Once we identify the flaws in our innate patterns of upbringing and culture, we can let them go, and move into a new way of being, one in alignment with who we really are.

6. **Release the past.** Without forgiveness and gratitude, we will never be free. Release those who have hurt us. Love is waiting on the other side!

7. **Trust in the process.** We are where we are for a reason, and it takes what it takes for us to change. Everything we do is a stepping-stone to what happens next. You are standing in exactly the right place for you.

8. **Clarify intentions.** We can't expect others to support our dreams if we haven't voiced them to ourselves. clear expectations are both empowering and an effective tool of success. The truth is, we don't have to sell out our souls in the process of building a career!

9. **Never stay for the money.** The longer we stay where we do not belong because of financial insecurity, the harder it is on our bodies and souls.

10. **Find your soul's purpose.** Where in your life are you holding back? Where do you have the most fear around making a change? Is there an action you long to take, yet can't imagine taking? that way lies gold. If we become open and teachable, the right teachers will come.

11. **Everyone is a gift.** We're all constantly beaming information back and forth, absorbing lessons and offering them back. It's no accident who or what comes into our sphere of influence. We land in each other's life for a reason.

12. **Seek like-minded souls.** Find your own tribe of loving colleagues who can nurture your strengths and help keep you honest.

13. **Practice willingness (stay teachable).** Only when we are open to learning and growing does Spirit have room to do her work! Willingness is the prerequisite to transformation.

14. **Lead with love.** There is no more powerful tool for change. Business is relationships. When there is more space for the human spirit in the equation, the results are rewarding, productive, and profitable. Within each of us lies the power to transform relationships by leading with love. All we have to do is open our hearts.

15. **Do the inner work.** This is the only path to true transformation. Self-confidence is not an attitude—it's an inside job first and foremost. Unless we've done this work, we will never be open to change, or realize our fullest potential.

16. **Change wanting into welcoming in.** One has its roots in lack and fear, the other floats in a sea of abundance. Choose abundance!

17. **Balance masculine and feminine energies.** All of us need to honor and embody both male and female energy to stay in balance, to use all of what we are. Neither one is right or wrong—done with integrity and love, Integrating both approaches are a divine way to be, and the truest path to finding our souls in success.

Bonus tools:
18. **Keep your sense of humor.** Where would we be without laughter? When we take ourselves too seriously, the world becomes dull indeed. Humor is healing, and uplifts us all. as my friend Robert White once said, Save the earth—it's the only planet with chocolate on it.

19. **Be additive.** Try entering situations with an expectation of offering, as opposed to receiving. Vernan Jordan put it best—We exist temporarily through what we take, but we live forever through what we give.

20. **Be truthful. Be gentle. Be fearless.** Gandhi's words speak for themselves. I leave you with them, along with my heartfelt wish that these tools help you build a strong ladder that can lead you to your wildest dreams.

GRATITUDE FROM KATHY

I am grateful for my son, Leo, who has been so loving and supportive of my journey in life, and in starting Qualis International.

My granddaughter Alyssa, and her mother Tammy who are a constant inspiration for me.

My parents and brothers for all of the many lessons and joy! All of my colleagues at The World Business Academy for so many years, who always reflected back to me truth, integrity, ethics and spirituality in business.

Friends that have allowed me to grow and learn the most important life's lessons, in the most loving and unique ways: Jerry Cohn, David Strauss, George and Karen McCown, Rinaldo Brutoco, Willis Harman, Jim Cusumano, Brian Chossak, Deepak Chopra, Jean Houston, Joan Borysenko, Bruce Lipton, Lynne Twist, Rosie Lazzeri, Paul McGuckin, and Pete Carroll.

There are so many others to whom I am thankful; for their kindness, friendship, love and support… you know who you are!

To my wonderful co-writer, Tinker Lindsay, who brought my stories alive with love, humor and grace! I am deeply grateful!

GRATITUDE FROM TINKER

First and foremost, thanks to Kathy Gardarian, for trusting me with her story, and inviting me to relay her fascinating vision for finding spirit in success. It takes both faith and courage to let someone else give voice to your deepest truths, and I am so grateful to Kathy for allowing me to do so. This collaboration has forged a new friendship, and the project has been a powerful catalyst for insight, growth, and joy.

Big thanks, too, to Jim Cusumano for intuiting that Kathy and I might click as collaborators. Good matchmaking, sir!

I drew inspiration from several books—notably *I will not die an unlived life*, by Dawna Markova—and am grateful for all the magnificent memoirists and inspirational authors who have paved new paths and empowered readers like me with their brave truth-telling.

Deep appreciation to my agent, Andrea Cavallaro at The Sandra Dijkstra Literary Agency, for mid-wifing this book. She's a wiz with contracts and all things literary, but it's her wicked humor that makes working with her such a delight.

Love and gratitude to my ever-expanding family that currently includes five grandchildren—Addie, Daisy, Jack, Gus, and Iris. I can't imagine this world, not to mention my life, without them. I shall do my very best to preserve our wondrous planet so that these guardians of our future have a safe and healthy home in which to thrive.

Finally, of course, huge love and thanks to my husband Cameron. He is my perfect foil, partner, playmate and friend. I wake up beside him every morning and think, Lucky me.

WISDOM SAMPLER FROM KATHY'S LIBRARY

The Seven Spiritual Laws of Success: a pocketbook guide to Fulfilling Your Dreams—Deepak Chopra

Balance: The Business-Life Connection—James Cusumano

Be Here Now—Ram Dass

Wisdom of The Ages: 60 days to enlightenment—Wayne Dyer

Global Mind Change: the promise of the 21st Century—Willis Harman

The Passion of Isis and Osiris: A Gateway to Transcendent Love—Jean Houston, Ph.D.

The Biology of Belief: Unleashing the Power of Consciousness, Matter and Miracles—Bruce H. Lipton, Ph.D.

I Will Not Die an Unlived Life: Reclaiming Passion and Purpose—Dawna Markova

The One Life We're Given: Finding the Wisdom That Waits in Your Heart—Mark Nepo

The Power of Now: A Guide to Spiritual Enlightenment—Eckhart Tolle

Living an Extraordinary Life—Robert White

ABOUT THE AUTHORS

Kathleen M. Gardarian

Kathy Gardarian is the Founder and CEO of Qualis International Inc., a multi-million dollar sales and distribution company. She has served as a director on many boards, both corporate and non-profit, including Van's Inc., The World Business Academy, Chapman University, The Gorbachov State of the World Forum, and the Woman's Leadership Board at Harvard's JFK School. She was awarded the Lifetime Achievement Award from the National Association of Woman Business Owners, and has been one of the top forty woman-owned businesses in Orange County in Southern California. She lives in Newport Coast, California.

Kathy is available to speak to groups concerning this subject.

www.thewisdomofloveinbusiness.com

Tinker Lindsay

A member of Writers Guild of America (WGA), Independent Writers of Southern California (IWOSC), Women in Film (WIF), and Mystery Writers of America (MWA), Tinker Lindsay has been a passionate collaborator and dedicated transformational storyteller for over three decades.

She is co-author, along with best-selling author Gay Hendricks, of the popular Rule of Ten series, featuring ex-monk, ex-cop, Los Angeles-based Private Investigator Tenzing Norbu, and published by Hay House Visions. She wrote *Milton's Secret*, a YA novelization of the film based on the children's book by Eckhart Tolle and Robert S. Freidman, and has worked with transformational authors including Peter Russell, Arjuna Ardagh, John C. Robinson, Anne Bertolet Rice, and Dara Marks.

Tinker Lindsay has written screenplays for major studios, collaborating with award-winning film director and primary screen-writing partner, Peter Chelsom. Recent film projects include *Hector and the Search for Happiness*, starring Simon Pegg and Rosamund Pike. She co-wrote the spiritual epic *Buddha: The Inner Warrior* with acclaimed Indian director Pan Nalin (*Samsara, Faith Connections, Angry Indian Goddesses*), and *Annie Cook* with Cameron Keys.

Lindsay graduated with high honors from Harvard University in English and American Language and Literature. She has four grown children and five beautiful grandchildren. She can usually be found writing in her home office, situated directly under the Hollywood sign.